D0555046

EATiQuette's[SM]

the main course on TABLE SERVICE

SKILLS & TIPS
for becoming a
- **CONFIDENT**
- **EFFICIENT**
- **PROFESSIONAL**
  SERVER

BY
David Rothschild

Copyright © 2001 David and Barbara Rothschild
All rights reserved.
No part of this book may be reproduced, stored in a retrieval
system, or transmitted by any means, electronic, mechanical,
photocopying, recording, or otherwise, without
written permission from the author.

For more information on
EATiQuette^{SM} publications and services:
2238 East Wahalla Lane
Phoenix, AZ 85024-1260
Phone: 602-569-2051
Fax: 602-765-1746
E-mail: info@EATiQuette.com
Web site: www.EATiQuette.com

ISBN 1-59113-042-5

Table of Contents

Special thanks to . . .

. . . *BJ and Gilbert Hernandez, owners of the Havana Cafés in Phoenix and Scottsdale, Arizona, for providing the location, tablewares, equipment and food for the photographs in this book and for being such good friends for so many years.*

. . . *Havana Patio Café server **Hilario Salgado** for agreeing to be featured on the cover and for his kind and skilled assistance during our photo shoot.*

. . . *Marlene Hannsberry, Mary Taylor, Carol Rothschild, Barb Silvestro, Bill Gadzia, Nancy Russell and Eric Fischer for reading this manual in its pre-production stages. Your feedback and input definitely helped to make this a more accurate, educational and entertaining book. I truly appreciate your time and efforts.*

. . . *Carl Letsch, for bringing the idea of writing this book from my subconscious to my conscious thoughts and for your continued support of both my individual endeavors and the MetroTech Culinary Arts Department.*

. . . *my wife, **Barbara**, without whom this book would never have been written. Her encouragement, contributions, editing and writing helped to transform this book from my biographical musings into a readable textbook.*

The Main Course on Table Service

Chapter 1

Who is David Rothschild?...

I started my career, as did many Jewish boys from Brooklyn, in the Catskill Mountains of New York. I tell people that I grew up in the restaurant business. Actually, I was *born* into the restaurant business. When my mother was pregnant with me, my dad was the attorney for, and part owner of, a resort hotel. Some of my earliest memories are of crawling around in the cavernous kitchens and I've always loved the sounds and smells of these large, active production facilities.

Both of my older brothers worked as waiters to put themselves through college. I eagerly awaited my turn and, at 15, got my first hospitality job as a bellman at a resort hotel where my brother was Maître d' in the dining room.

The following summer, I became a waiter. The guests would arrive at the resort on Sunday and I'd have them in my station for a week or more, serving them three meals a day. They could have anything they wanted, as much as they wanted. Their meals were included in the cost of the lodging. This is known as the "American Plan".

After the first few weeks, I was hooked. I found that I had a talent for service. I loved the interaction. I enjoyed pleasing the guests. I *really* enjoyed the money!

I financed my college education by working summers at the resort. By eighteen, I had my own apartment. I lived by myself and made enough money during the summers that I didn't have to work all winter.

After obtaining a BA Degree, I branched out into other areas of sales (who can deny that a server's job is, at least in part, sales?) and tried my hand at technical writing before coming to Phoenix in 1976. A classified ad redirected me to food service and I became a waiter at the Arizona Biltmore Hotel, one of the *grande dame* resorts in the State.

As the Phoenix fine dining scene grew and prospered, I volleyed from server to manager to food and beverage director at some of the area's finest properties. I was on the opening team of the Registry Resort in Scottsdale and the Hassayampa in Prescott, Arizona. When the Valley's restaurants and resorts literally shut down for the blistering summers, I took my skills on the road and worked at the world-renowned Broadmoor Hotel in Colorado Springs, Colorado, the private and exclusive Little Harbor Club in Harbor Springs, Michigan and the Mescalero Apache owned-and-operated Inn of the Mountain Gods in Ruidoso, New Mexico.

I've had the good fortune of working with some of the Southwest's premier chefs including Vincent Guerithault of Vincent's on Camelback (named 1993 James Beard Foundation's Best Chef Southwest) and Erasmo "Razz" Kamnitzer, who's regularly featured on TV Food Network shows and whose restaurant has been named one of *Esquire Magazine's* Top 25 in the U.S.

Somewhere along the way, I realized that I'd found a career and had been unaware of it! I was making a good living, setting my own hours, and really enjoying the work.

I've also gotten to meet, and learn from, some fascinating people throughout my years in the business. Former co-workers have gone on to other wonderful careers when they were finished with restaurant service. A fellow server wrote a screenplay that was later made into a movie starring Gene Wilder. I spotted a buddy from a Catskill Mountains resort on TV as a lead lawyer in front of the U.S. Senate during an investigation.

I've had the opportunity, while working in fine dining rooms, to have served then-President Gerald Ford, Bob Hope and Johnny Carson as well as many other celebrities. Part of my Assistant Maître d' duties at a showroom was to look after the needs of the performers. I served Ella Fitzgerald hot tea between shows in her dressing room. B.B. King preferred a snifter of Cognac. I assisted Sly Stallone in throwing a surprise birthday party for his then-girlfriend, Susan Anton.

I've worked private clubs where the guests' surnames were Armstrong, Ford, Swift, Lambert and others – the corporate wealth of America. They were, to a one, courteous to me and to the servers. A sign of gentility is being kind and generous to those who serve you. They knew that.

In 1988, I accepted a position as Service Instructor in a high school Culinary Arts Program. I also accepted about half of the pay that I had been making in industry! I became a teacher, but am still a restaurateur. Only now, I operate restaurants with teenagers (not so very different than the staffs in the restaurants where I do training workshops). As a culinary arts instructor, I develop curriculum for, and operate, a program that's one of only two in the State of Arizona.

My wife, Barbara, and I formed our own company, EATiQuette^{SM}, in 1998. We've presented service training and dining etiquette seminars for groups and businesses all across the country. We write a weekly newspaper column on dining etiquette and offer etiquette tips on our web site at www.EATiQuette.com.

I've spent the better part of four decades in the food service industry. I've owned my own restaurant where I did all of the cooking. I'm *not*, however, a chef, though I'm a pretty fair cook – just ask my wife or any number of chefs I've cooked for. What I *am* is a gracious host, welcoming each of my restaurant guests as though they were dining in my own home. That's the role I've chosen to play in the restaurant business, and the one that gives me the most personal and financial satisfaction.

. . . and why did he write this book?

There's a lot of good food out there right now and there's a greater respect for the American chef than at perhaps any other time in American culinary history.

When I first started in the restaurant business in the early '60s, the only great chefs were European. The finest restaurants in large U.S. cities stole their Executive Chefs from the great French, Austrian and German kitchens.

Chefs in the United States today set culinary trends, they don't follow them. There has become a kind of International Cuisine; a fusing of elements and techniques from around the globe. It's not at all unusual for a chef in Phoenix to serve a *poblano* chile stuffed with Jamaican-style curried goat and drizzled with a French *Beurre Blanc* sauce.

Service is the last frontier

With all of the strides we've made in our restaurant kitchens, service in the United States has not kept up with the food preparation.

I believe that superior service has to be a part of the package that makes a meal memorable.

Everywhere I go, people criticize the state of table service. I hear it from customers. I hear it from owners. I even hear it from servers.

A recent National Restaurant Association survey found that more than 60% of all complaints in restaurants were about service. I've seen many restaurants that served outstanding food close their doors when customers stopped coming, due to the inept service. I've also experienced restaurants that serve adequate food along with warm, friendly, professional service. These are the ones that continue to prosper.

This book is written for all of the restaurant managers who want a concise, straightforward way to teach service to their staff. It's easy! Restaurant service is *not* rocket science.

This book is also written for all of those servers out there who have decided to make service a career, or who just want to make more money at what they're already doing.

This book is written for, and dedicated to, those of you who believe, as I do, that the service a restaurant provides is *at least* as important as the food that it serves.

Let's take a look at some of the legends who established formal cuisine and helped shape American fine dining as we know it . . .

Chapter 2

Culinary legends:
some of the chefs and hosts
who shaped the industry

Quantity cooking has been around since the earliest recorded history. The Bible is full of examples of multi-course meals. The epic poem, *The Iliad,* by Homer (8th century BC), has wonderful examples of the enormous quantities of food required to serve the various armies. There's a recipe for cooking a whole ostrich (a food source that's having a resurgence today) in the earliest surviving cookbook, *Apicius; Cookery and Dining in Imperial Rome*, by Marcus Gabius Apicius, who lived sometime between 80 BC and 40 AD.

Antonin Carême (1784-1833) and Auguste Escoffier (1847-1935) are the two most influential names in classical cuisine.

Carême was hailed as *"Cuisnier des rois et le roi des cuisniers"* – "The cook of kings and the king of cooks." He's thought of as the father of classic French cookery. Carême wrote many books on the subjects of stocking the pantry, choosing only the freshest ingredients, categorizing major and minor sauces, and standardizing the spelling of many dishes.[1]

In 1890, Escoffier, in association with César Ritz, helped to open the Savoy Hotel in London. He is considered by many to be the

father of modern cooking. Escoffier is credited with simplifying French cuisine and bringing order to the French kitchen. The system he devised, *Brigade de Cuisine* (the staff of the kitchen), is still in use today.[2] We generally refer to it as the classical kitchen hierarchy.

When "bussing" was more than clearing tables . . .

Etienne Gluck, one of Phoenix's best-known maître d's, was famous for his gentility and classic French mannerisms, one of which was his habit of "bussing" ladies' hands as they entered the restaurant. He'd take the lady's hand and lightly touch his lips to it. While this may seem extremely outdated, in its day it was considered a very respectable ~ and respectful ~ way to greet a female guest.

In the history of elegant hotels, the name César Ritz (1850-1918) has become synonymous with excellence. Consider the term "ritzy" and the words posh, expensive, sophisticated and luxurious come to mind. He insisted that everything be of the highest quality. Ritz's philosophy that "The customer is always right," has been the catch phrase of the hospitality industry for most of the last century.[3]

Perhaps the most famous restaurateur at the turn of the 20th Century was Oscar Tschirky (and, no, I'm *not* sure how his name is pronounced). He was known as, "Oscar of the Waldorf".

Tschirky introduced America to the concept of the Head Waiter, or *Maître d'* (an abbreviated form of *Maître d'Hôtel*, or Master of the Hotel). He came to symbolize all that the Waldorf stood for. He was sophisticated, genteel, and knew how to deal with his rich and famous clientele. He built the customer base with his charm and his tableside preparations. Tschirky is credited with creating the Waldorf Salad, as well as Veal Oscar.[4]

Oscar of the Waldorf was the first "front man" for a restaurant in the United States. Guests returned to the Waldorf not so much for the food as for the pampering that they received from Oscar and his staff. He was so well-known during the 1940s that Edward Keane portrayed him in the classic movie *Sergeant York*.

Other movies of that era also depicted the restaurant maître d' as a suave, sophisticated and well-respected host. It's worth checking out, for example, Charles Boyer's charming, confident head waiter character in *History Is Made At Night* (1937).

In Stanley Tucci's *The Big Night* (1996), Tucci himself plays a restaurateur who uses both his wits and charisma to try to save his failing 1950s Italian restaurant.

Today, you'll still find a few famous hosts in big city dining establishments. Among them, Chicago's Arturo Petterino is legendary. As the long-time maître d' of the Pump Room, Petterino played host to Hollywood stars, local and national politicians and well-known socialites. He became so much a part of the city's culinary scene that, in early 2001, the Lettuce Entertain You restaurant group opened a fine dining venue, Petterino's, in his honor and persuaded the masterful maître d' to come out of retirement to schmooze its guests. Sirio Maccioni of Le Cirque (New York and Las Vegas) is another restaurant host who operates in the classic style. Having trained at some of the finest hotels in Europe, Maccioni learned at an early age not only fine dining service, but also dining room diplomacy – recognizing his glamorous guests as they sweep through the door and giving them the treatment to which they feel they're entitled. Both Mr. Petterino and Mr. Maccioni have been featured on the TV Food Network's "Legendary Hangouts" series.

Unfortunately though, in the 21st century, you'd be hard-pressed to find many American restaurants that are known for their front-of-house personalities. This is the era of celebrity chefs, and they're the ones taking on the task of entertaining and ensuring that their guests enjoy a pleasant dining experience. Some spend as much (or more) time in the dining room as they do in the kitchen. When they're knowledgeable about service and have the skills of a good host, the restaurant benefits. When they're *not* . . . well, the restaurant suffers.

To paraphrase an old hospitality text, many special restaurateurs were born in hamlets or on farms. The simplicity, hospitality and honesty taught them in their homes were the fundamental principles used in their dealings with their customers. These people weren't just customers, they were neighbors.[5]

Conrad Hilton, one of the world's foremost hoteliers, once said: "The thing I have liked best about the hotel business is the fun of being the host. I've always liked having people around me; people never fail to fascinate me."[6]

There's much to be learned from historic hosts like César Ritz, Oscar Tschirky and Conrad Hilton. Their genuine concern for their guests is a characteristic of every good server, whether he's working in the local diner or a five-star restaurant.

To best serve your guests, it's important to understand how a restaurant runs and the various roles, in both front- and back-of-house that make up the whole . . .

Chapter 3

The culinary cast and crew:
front and back of "house"
("house" refers to the restaurant, as a whole)

A restaurant is often compared to the theater. The "back-of-house" in the theater consists of all of the people behind the scenes; lighting crew, set builders, lighting and sound engineers and costume designers.

The "back-of-house" in a restaurant setting consists of those people with little or no customer contact: the chefs, cooks, apprentices, and dishwashers. Of course, with the advent of exhibition kitchens and celebrity chefs, we're seeing a lot more of these people nowadays.

We'll talk about "front-of-house" as it relates to both restaurant and theater later on in the chapter.

Where are the monkey dishes?
(a "monkey dish", by the way, is a small bowl sometimes used for sides or dressings)

In a vacation destination like Phoenix, there's an abundance of resort hotels. When a server is confronted, for the first time, with the structure of a resort kitchen (or any classically-structured large kitchen, for that matter) it can be bewildering. *Who's in charge?*

Who do I ask for what I need? Once you learn the positions in the kitchen, you'll have a much better idea of who does what and how they relate to what you do . . .

Here's a flow chart of a typical **Back-of-House**:

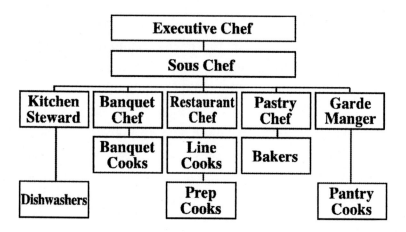

Back of House Job Descriptions

Executive Chef - the manager responsible for all aspects of food production in the hotel, including menu planning, purchasing, costing and planning work schedules. Rarely does any of the hands-on cooking. In the best scenario, teaches the new cooks while doing rounds of the various kitchen stations.

Sous *(Soo)* **Chef** - directly in charge of production and the minute-to-minute supervision of the staff. Carries out the Executive Chef's orders for the day.

Restaurant Chef - day to day operation of the restaurant. Responsible for his staff and for quality control.

HOT STATIONS - The Line Cooks:

Saucier *(saw-see-AY)* - prepares stocks, soups and sauces and sautés foods to order. This is usually the highest position of the station chefs.

Broiler Cook - handles all of the broiled items, steaks, chops, etc. In most operations, also responsible for all roasted meat preparations.

Fry Cook - responsible for all of the deep frying items on the menu. In many operations, also in charge of all vegetable preparations.

COLD STATIONS:

Garde Manger *(gard mahn-JHAY)* **or Pantry Cook** - French term for "Guardian of cold meats". Responsible for the cold foods, including salads, dressings and sandwiches. Also responsible for cold hors d'oeuvres and buffet presentations including ice carvings and *chaud froids* (elaborately-decorated, aspic-glazed presentations of poultry, seafood or game). Often one of the most artistic people in the kitchen.

Pastry Chef - supervises the pastry department, makes out the dessert menus, decorates cakes and special pastries.

Chef Tournant *(tour-NAHNT)* **or Swing Cook** - relief cook, replaces other station heads on their day off. Usually must cover a different job each day of the week.

Other Traditional Kitchen Positions

Banquet Chef - in charge of all parties. Supervises the preparation of all of the party foods. Under the direct supervision of the Executive Chef.

Butcher - responsible for boning, cutting and preparing all beef, pork, lamb, veal for cooking. May also be responsible for cutting and preparing fish and poultry for cooking.

Baker - the head baker bakes all breads, rolls and quick breads. Responsible for the operation of the bakery, but is generally under the supervision of the pastry chef.

Breakfast Cook - prepares hot cereals and is responsible for all of the breakfast orders. In many operations, will also be the fry cook during lunch.

Prep Cook (hot side of the kitchen) - washes, peels, cleans and cuts vegetables, which will later be used by the chefs.

Pantry Cook (cold side of the kitchen) - washes, peels, cleans and prepares vegetables for use in salads, sandwiches and cold buffets.

Kitchen Steward - manager who is responsible for the organization of the kitchen smallwares (serving pieces, serving trays, flatware, etc.). Supervises all dish washers and pot washers. Inventories and stores platewares, flatwares and specialty utensils. Truly one of the most important people in the kitchen. *You want the Kitchen Steward on your side!*

Dish Washer/Pot Washer – responsible for receiving, sorting, scraping and washing all dishes, glasses, flatware and, often, cooking pots, pans and utensils. Returns clean wares to their appropriate storage locations. May sometimes perform some Prep Cook duties as well. Works under the supervision of the Kitchen Steward. As many chefs will tell you, you can't run a restaurant without a dishwasher.

To continue the theater/restaurant comparison, the "front-of-house" in the theater consists of the actors and actresses – those people who appear in public.

The "front-of-house" in a restaurant setting is all of those people who have contact with the customers: the maître d', host/hostess, cashier, sommelier/wine steward, captain, waiters and assistant waiters/bussers.

Here's a flow chart of the typical Front-of-House in several different types of food service situations:

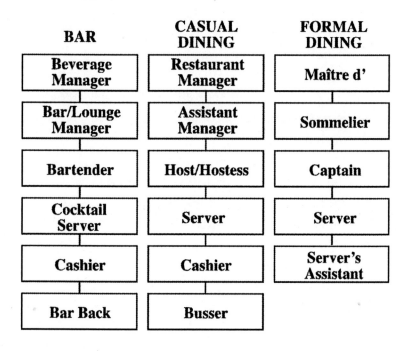

BAR	CASUAL DINING	FORMAL DINING
Beverage Manager	Restaurant Manager	Maître d'
Bar/Lounge Manager	Assistant Manager	Sommelier
Bartender	Host/Hostess	Captain
Cocktail Server	Server	Server
Cashier	Cashier	Server's Assistant
Bar Back	Busser	

Front of House - Job Descriptions

Maître d'Hôtel *(usually referred to as the Maître d', pronounced "MAY-treh DEE" or "MAY-ter DEE")* - person in charge of the dining room in a hotel or restaurant. Charged with hiring, training and supervising the dining room staff. Supervises day to day operation of the restaurant. Must be well-groomed and have a good working knowledge of foods and wines. Reports directly to the Food & Beverage Director or General Manager.

Host/Hostess - greets guests as they enter the dining room. Escorts guests to the tables and presents menus. Answers the phone and takes reservations per the Maître d's instructions. Directs guests to the various facilities and must be able to answer guests' questions about the establishment.

Captain - in charge of a section of the dining room and the leader of a service team. Suggests daily specials to the patrons and answers any questions regarding the menu. Takes the order and gives it to the waiter for the kitchen to prepare. Assists in the service of the food. May suggest and serve wine to the patrons.

Sommelier *(SUM-uhl-YAY, so-muh-LYAY)* **or Wine Steward** - needs to be very knowledgeable about wines and after-dinner liqueurs. Assists patrons in the selection of wines to complement their food choices, presents and serves the wines they've selected. In very formal dining rooms, may also offer cognacs, after dinner drinks and fine cigars.

Waiter/Waitress or Server - serves food and beverages to guests. Takes the order in less formal restaurants. Sets the tables, assists in bussing and resetting tables. May process the guest check, or handle the check between the guest and cashier.

Server's Assistant or Busser - assists the waiter by performing a variety of functions: bussing (removing finished courses and used dishes), serving beverages and refilling water and beverage

Don't "dis" the dishwasher ...

As a server, the more friends you have in the kitchen, the easier your job is going to be. If you treat all of the kitchen staff ~ from executive chef to the dishwashers ~ with respect and are polite (remember your "pleases" and "thank yous"), you'll be more likely to get cooperation when you need something "on the fly" for that order you forgot to place with the kitchen.

glasses, bread and butter service. Removes and replaces soiled linen and resets tables.

Cashier - issues checks to the waitstaff. Receives guest checks and payments from servers or from departing guests, in less formal restaurants. Enters on the POS (point of sale) system, computer or cash register the amount indicated on the check. Makes change or finalizes a credit card transaction. Responsible to the Controller or the Auditor.

Bar Manager - in charge of all of the alcoholic beverage service in a facility. Responsible for hiring, training, scheduling and inventory control.

Bartender - greets guests as they enter the bar, takes their orders, mixes and serves the alcoholic drinks. May receive payment and make change. Responsible for the appearance of the bar and for seeing that sufficient supplies are on hand.

Cocktail Server - takes the guests' orders and serves the beverages prepared by the bartender. Collects payment from the guests. At times, may suggest and describe various cocktails or wines.

Bar Back - Helper for the bartenders. Carries supplies and equipment such as fruits, soft drinks, paper goods and ice to the bartender. Assists in washing glasses and in general clean-up duties.

AT THE HELM OF THE "HOUSE": Food & Beverage Director - The person in this position is in charge of all of a property's food service operations. All food and beverage personnel, including the executive chef, restaurant and bar managers report to the "F&B", as they're known in the business. Sometimes, in smaller resorts and restaurants, this position is filled by the General Manager.

Now you have a basic understanding of who does what in the food service operation. But who *are* the people who choose to make a living in the service segment of this business? Read on . . .

Chapter 4

Service as a career ... and a lifestyle

Restaurant service in the United States is not generally thought of as a glamorous or highly sought-after career. Many waiters, when asked what they do, say, "I work in a restaurant." In Europe, though, waiters are given extensive training and often have to apprentice for a number of years. There, service is considered an honorable and respected trade.

Here, it's usually a way to support yourself until the "right" job comes along. Most servers I've worked with over the years never think of what they're doing as a career. They just happened onto restaurant service after having tried other jobs.

There are more service jobs available than ever before. More than 5.4 million people held jobs in food and beverage service in 1998, the most recent year for which statistics are available. Waiter/waitress positions accounted for more than 2 million; bartenders more than 400,000, and hosts/hostesses more than 400,000. By 2006, total restaurant employment (both front and back of house) is expected to increase to a record 12 million.[7]

Service is *not* for everyone

I've met very few chefs, for example, who are comfortable dealing with customers. They'd rather be in the kitchen.

There are certainly drawbacks to this career choice . . .

To this day, many restaurants don't offer medical, dental or retirement plans. This puts you in a similar position to someone who's self-employed, since it's up to you to provide insurance protection for yourself and your family and plan for your financial future.

If you *have* chosen a career in service you're on a different schedule than most other people. You *don't* have a 9-to-5 job. You'll probably work Friday and Saturday nights – and most holidays. I worked every New Year's Eve of my adult life until I started teaching. If you have seniority in a restaurant, you probably have Sunday and Monday as your days off.

Relationships are difficult to maintain. You and your significant other probably work different shifts and don't see each other very often. Getting together for meals can be difficult, so this doesn't happen often in a "restaurant" family.

Restaurant service *does* have its advantages . . .

You *don't* work a 9-to-5 job. You *don't* sit at a desk all day doing the same boring things over and over. Every shift is different. You meet interesting people every day, most of them surprisingly nice (*no*, the majority of your guests *won't* treat you like their slave). You work in a clean, air-conditioned environment. When I'm finished with my shift, I rarely think about my job. I don't take work "home from the office" with me.

You're surrounded by quick-witted, intelligent people. Restaurant servers are some of the brightest, most fun people I've ever known. Chances are that, as a server, your circle of friends will include others in the business, not only fellow servers, but chefs and restaurant owners. After a few years in the business, you're likely to know (from having worked with or for them, or having served them) some of the most influential people in your area.

Save in the busy season ~ here's the reason . . .

My friend and fellow waiter, Dennis, recently overheard a conversation between some young co-workers. They were stressing over what they'd do for money during the summer, when there are fewer shifts and their tips would decrease dramatically. Dennis admitted to me, not to them, that it took him ten years to realize that he had to set money aside for the slow season. Let that be a lesson to you, servers!

There's a great deal of immediate gratification in doing your job well. When a guest leaves my station having had a great dining experience, it makes me very proud. I know that a large part of the credit goes to me and to my service team.

Let's not discount the financial aspect of the job. A waiter in a good restaurant typically works from 5 to 11 PM, though shifts vary greatly, depending on the hours and volume of business. A good waiter in a good "house" in New York, for example, will make $75,000 a year or more.

It's not difficult to earn a good living waiting tables.

When you work for tips you're, in a sense, an entrepreneur – the amount of money you make is dependent on the initiative you show and how well you present yourself and your restaurant to your guests. Let's talk a little more about the tipping tradition and how to make the best of the fact that your income is so dependent on the whims of the public.

First, what *are* tips?

Tips is an acronym. It stands for:
To
Insure
Prompt
Service

(okay, grammatically, it's to *ensure* prompt service, but you get the point!)

Tipping isn't mandatory. Nor is it a city in China, as the old restaurant joke goes. It *is*, however, a longstanding custom in the United States. In Europe and many parts of the Caribbean, the tip is usually added directly to the guest check. In Japan, tipping is not generally expected unless some extra service has been performed. Until recently in China, it was inappropriate to tip. Times are changing there but, even now, only a 3% tip is the norm (and it's often appreciated if that tip is paid in U.S. dollars). In Hong Kong, servers expect at least 10% on top of any service charge that's levied. In Australia, some restaurants have a no-tipping policy, at others, the standard is 10%.

There's a difference, though, between tips and service charges. Tips are intended solely for the service team. Service charges may be distributed any way that management feels is fair. In some cases, a portion of a service charge goes to the kitchen employees, who don't otherwise work for tips.

Throughout my career, most of my two-week paychecks were for this amount: $0.00. Very few servers are paid the standard minimum wage. Because of their profession, most are paid an hourly rate of just $2.20, or thereabouts (Yes, this is legal, since it's assumed that they'll make up the rest in tips). By the time your taxes and any medical payments are deducted, your meager paycheck has disappeared.

When I work as a server, I never look at individual tips. It doesn't really make any sense to do that since it all averages out in the long run. If I peek and see a good tip (18% or higher), it momentarily pleases me. If I look and see a poor tip (less than 15%), it's going to upset me and I'll lose focus on the other tables I have to serve. And, in the grand scheme of things, what does it matter?

I do suggest that you keep a log of your tips and, at the end of the month, take a look at the total. If you're happy with what you've made, great. If not, it's time to look for a new job.

Think you can spot a poor tipper?

You might be surprised!

At one very nice restaurant where I worked, two business women were having dinner. Aaah . . . women ~ poor tippers you might say to yourself. Well, they spent $1,100 on dinner that night and left the service team a $200 tip. So much for that stereotype!

Never assume, from the looks of people, what tip they'll leave you.

Living on tips can be challenging. Many a time I've stopped by the neighborhood tavern or all-night diner with some of the crew to unwind from the shift. When I'd get home and enter my total into my "tip ledger" it wasn't at all unusual for the cash in my pocket to be only half of what I'd made that night. It's too easy to spend money when you have it on hand. Just ask my nephew whose earnings from his job as a server at a local Mexican restaurant have so far gone toward a DVD player, a memory card for his MP3 player . . . but not a penny toward the car that he says he's saving up for.

What you need to keep in mind, with all that cash burning a hole in your pocket, is that you *can't* count on a paycheck to cover your bills. You have to set aside money for your rent, mortgage, utilities, car payment . . .

And set a little aside, too, to treat the chefs to a drink or a cup of coffee next time they join you after the shift. Chefs are notorious for not having cash – and servers always do. Consider this another way to improve relations between front and back of house.

I've heard young waiters say, "I sure don't see myself doing this when I'm 50 years old." Well, you don't *have* to. Restaurant service is definitely not a dead-end career. There are lots of things that you can do after you've had a successful career as a server, often while staying in the food service industry.

Many servers go into restaurant management. Hotels, resorts and country clubs provide many opportunities to move up the career ladder. They'll often pay for you to go to school if you choose to continue your education. The larger hotel chains offer management schools and classes once you've been with the organization for a length of time. Servers can eventually become Food & Beverage Directors or General Managers of hotel restaurants.

Many servers also choose to go into the banquet side of the business to become catering and sales managers. They start up their own businesses or work for independent caterers. Some go into other areas of tourism, working for convention and visitors' bureaus, air and cruise lines. Many open their own restaurants. Still others, like myself, become teachers or restaurant consultants.

Often, servers are recruited by automobile dealerships and insurance companies for their sales abilities. There are many things you can pursue if and when you become tired of waiting tables.

Let's look at some of the qualifications and qualities of a good server . . .

Chapter 5

Fourteen qualities of every good server ~ and one all-important rule

Waiters and waitresses come in all sizes, shapes and colors.

When I lived in New York many years ago, it was said that, at one time or another, everyone in the five boroughs had worked as a cab driver. I think that today, with the proliferation of restaurants, almost everyone has worked as a server sometime in his life.

So what qualities do you need to be successful in service?

Reliable - Be at your job every day. I taught for three years without taking one sick day. Since I worked for tips for so many years, my mindset was, "You don't work, you don't make any money." It's not like working in an office – you can't have your "in-box" fill up and take care of it when you return the next day. If you aren't there, *someone* is doing your job for you.

Punctual - Be on time. The dining room is going to open whether you're there or not. A successful restaurant has to keep its posted hours. If you're not there, *someone* is covering your station. Quickly, everything gets out of whack because somebody else is covering your tables, they get overwhelmed, nobody knows who's in charge of which tables and the guests don't know who their server is.

Cooperative - Accept orders from your managers without arguing. Be willing to carry out tasks that have been assigned to you. Do your share of the work. Look for other tasks when you've finished yours. Try to get along with your co-workers (and remember . . . that includes the kitchen staff, too).

I'm often asked by human resource specialists to recommend an applicant for a service position. They rarely ask about technical skills. They want to know, "Does this person get along with fellow employees? Does he work well as part of a team? Is he able to accept criticism and grow from it? Can he keep an open mind?"

Flexible - Change is part of the business. Go with it. Sometimes you'll be asked to work extra hours; come in early, stay late. You may have to cancel plans because you've been called in to cover a shift for someone who's sick. You may show up one day and there's a new manager in charge, a new POS system has been installed, a new menu's in place. Be flexible. You can't always count on doing things the same way they've always been done – you need to adapt to the situation.

Thorough - Complete what you start. If a guest asks you to bring a birthday dessert for someone at the table, or asks a question about a dietary concern, you have to make sure these requests are handled promptly. You can ask a fellow employee to help, but you're ultimately responsible to see that it's done.

Organized - Concentrate on what you're doing – stay focused. As a server, you're always juggling a number of tasks. Learn to prioritize. Decide what needs to be done first, and do it.

Knowledgeable - Product knowledge is essential to the successful server. Know what you're talking about. Familiarize yourself with the menu. Ask the chef questions. If possible, taste the food. Learn about methods of preparation and cooking times.

Read a newspaper or watch TV news. It's important that a guest feels you're intelligent and know what's going on in the world.

Respect the knowledge of other employees and learn from them.

Learn about the company history. Familiarize yourself with the layout of the property. Be able to answer basic customer questions: "Is there a phone I can use?" "Where are the restrooms?"

Be aware of all company policies and adhere to them.

Ethical - Be truthful and honest. If there are blanks on your résumé, explain them the best way that you can. If you've made a mistake at the table, it's not a crime. It happens. Accept responsibility and own up to your mistakes. Your reputation in this business starts with your first job. Giving away food and drinks, or taking property that doesn't belong to you, is wrong. No, the boss may not miss that set of salt and pepper shakers that you're using at home, but there's always a chance that it'll get back to him or a future employer.

Sincere - We've all had a waiter approach the table with a plastered on smile and a "radio DJ" voice. Don't assume a different identity when you wait tables. You are who you are. Be professional, but be yourself at the table.

Loyal – Be respectful of the restaurant where you're currently employed. Don't "bad mouth" current or former employers or co-workers. The restaurant community is very tight knit. Your words are likely to come back to haunt you later on in your career. Remember, today's busser is tomorrow's restaurant manager – and you may be looking for a job.

Always try to give sufficient notice before leaving a position. Management may decide to "show you the door" immediately (it's happened to me) still, you've done the right thing.

Ambitious - Take initiative. Increase your knowledge of food and wine. Ask people in other jobs to teach you more about what they do – especially positions you might like to move into. Ask a server who makes good tips to give you some hints.

Personable - You have to *genuinely* like people to be a successful server. Be friendly, but not overly informal. We all have our bad days, but a good server is upbeat and cheerful and has a positive attitude.

Sense of Humor - A self-deprecating sense of humor can be a great asset. It has to be used sparingly, however. Inappropriate humor, or poorly timed humor can be disastrous. You never want to make the guest feel that he's the butt of your joke. I remember once early in my career, suggesting the lunch special of *Tongue Polonaise* to a guest. The guest replied, "*Me?* Eat something that came out of a cow's *mouth?*" My inappropriate comeback was, "So how did you enjoy your *eggs* this morning?" Neither he nor his guests was the least bit amused.

Professional –

A good server doesn't dress in the dining room. Don't go onto the restaurant floor until you're fully dressed in uniform. When you're putting on your apron or tying your tie as the guests are arriving, it appears that you're not ready for them – that's not very assuring for the diners. It's also not a good idea for staff members (especially while still in uniform) to be drinking at the bar or sitting in the dining room while service is still going on. While I'm on this subject, always wear appropriate attire when arriving and departing the restaurant. You, as an employee, are a reflection of your work place.

A good server doesn't eat or chew gum on the job. When you're on duty in the restaurant, refrain from all food and beverage consumption. Chewing gum is inappropriate at *all times* in a restaurant.

A good server doesn't carry pencils behind the ear. Or, for that matter, in the bun on top of your head! Don't remove the cap from a pen with your teeth or chew on your pencil. Depending on your uniform, writing implements should be kept in your vest or apron. That includes check holders and order pads, too – *never* jam them into your waistband, no matter how many servers you see with them tucked above their butts.

A good server is courteous. Use "please" and "thank you" when addressing both guests and co-workers. "No problem" is *not* a substitute for "you're welcome." Always put the guests' needs before your own. Give guests the right-of-way, even when you're in a hurry.

A good server is tactful. I tell servers to "be like Pagliacci." Remember that opera clown with a painted smile on his face? He was smiling on the outside but crying on the inside. Don't share problems with guests – they're in the restaurant to enjoy their meal, not to feel sorry for you. If you want to share anything, share the good stuff. Stay away from touchy subjects like politics and religion. Don't argue with the customer. Never assume the relationship between guests (for example, don't call a woman "Mrs." unless you know, for a fact, that the couple is married – to each other). Don't share information about one guest with another. *Never* correct a guests' pronunciation of a food or wine. Don't jump into the guests' conversation – you're not involved unless you've been asked to participate. Complaining or talking about guests while on the job is inappropriate. You never know who will hear and the conversation is likely to get back to the guest. A diner who overhears you talking about another guest has to wonder what you're saying about *him* when he's out of earshot.

There's a line that separates server from guest – don't step over it.

Lawns aren't the only place you'll find weeds . . .
You need to drop the drinks at table 2. Table 6 is waiting to give you their dessert order. The entrées for table 3 are still sitting in the pick-up window, but you have to take appetizer orders at table 5 before you can go into the kitchen. This is known as being "in the weeds" ~ having to juggle too many tasks at too many tables. Maybe it's because you spent too much time talking to a guest; maybe you're just not working efficiently. I have a friend whose nickname is "Weeds" because he always seems to be behind when he's serving. Staying organized and prioritizing tasks will help you stay "out of the weeds."

A good server acts the part.
Be poised and well-groomed. Carry an air of confidence. Take charge of your guests' dining experience. Make them feel comfortable and welcome, even in the most formal settings.

Avoid the appearance of being overwhelmed, though there are times when you will be. I recall working one evening when a water pipe burst in the kitchen. There must have been two inches of water on the floor. The guests didn't need to know about it – it wasn't their problem.

Do everything in a quiet and unrushed manner.

A good server is a good communicator. Develop a good speaking voice and a good command of the language. Don't use big words just for the sake of using them. Incorrect word usage is just plain embarrassing. Use words that you're familiar with.

A good server greets guests properly. Don't address guests by first name unless they specifically ask you to do so. Avoid slang and informality.

In formal situations, address guests as gentlemen or ladies; sir or madam (or ma'am) – *not* "folks." Say "Welcome," or "Good evening," not "Hi, how are ya?"

A good server keeps conversation with guests to a minimum. Be able to break off a conversation. This isn't always easy to do, but it's an important skill to learn. "Please excuse me, I'll be back in a minute. I have to check on an order." When guests see you spending too much time at one table, they think they're being neglected. Try to divide your time equally among your tables.

A good server doesn't speak in a loud voice, or quarrel with fellow employees. This is just unprofessional and can be upsetting for the guests. If you have the need to air grievances, do it outside, away from the dining room. If you can't resolve the problem, ask a manager to step in.

A good server is conscious of body language. Be aware of what your posture and movements say to others. We convey a lot of things without actually saying them. A graceful stride and stance indicate self-confidence and professionalism to the guest. But when your hands are in your pockets or you lean against the wall or chairs at the table, you're making a different statement to the guest and to management. You're saying that you'd rather be anywhere but here. You're bored.

Don't slouch at the table. Stand straight, leaning slightly forward to take a guest's order. A typical "at ease" posture for a server is hands clasped behind the back, attentive, with an "I'm here if you need me" look.

A server in an adjacent station asked me why, night after night, I always made better tips than he did. I asked him to examine his body language. He would approach the guest to take the order with his arms crossed in front of him. I mentioned to him that a crossed-armed stance was a very defensive posture. It says to the guest, "Don't give me a hard time, just give me your order."

A good server is always on the alert. You have to keep your eyes on your station, even when you're involved in a conversation. There's nothing wrong with conversing in a low tone with a fellow server, but you need to keep an eye on your station at all times. As a manager, I know that my servers aren't doing their jobs when guests are waving their hands all over the dining room! Don't stand in groups and *please*, don't congregate at the hostess or maître d' stand.

A good server never appears to be rushed or angry. There are times when you'll be both. The restaurant business can be frustrating and trying. But remember Pagliacci? Keep that smile on your face! Your guests don't need to know that you just spent five minutes screaming back and forth with the chef. Running in the dining room, kicking the kitchen door and slamming dishes into the bus box aren't going to make the situation any better.

The most important thing to remember as a server is this: ***Never* do anything that makes a guest feel uncomfortable, stupid or clumsy!**

Now you're thinking and acting like a pro, but do you *look* like one?

Chapter 6

The food looks great ~ do you?:
personal appearance and hygiene

The server is the person the guests will have the most contact with in the restaurant, so it's important that you observe the basics of good grooming and hygiene and always present a neat personal appearance.

Bathe daily - Sounds obvious doesn't it? We always have to be fresh-looking and polished. Make it a habit. Shower before every shift.

Use adequate antiperspirant/deodorant – Even if you don't usually use deodorant, do so when you have a shift in the restaurant. There are sudden changes in temperature between the dining rooms and the kitchens. You tend to perspire more at work than you do at home. You never want to have offending body odors. One of my least favorite duties as a manager is to pull a server aside and tell him that he has body odor. No one likes to hear that. No one likes to tell someone that.

Have clean teeth and fresh breath - Remember when you're taking the order, you're right in the guest's face. Be aware of your breath. If you're a coffee drinker or smoker, constantly refresh your breath. Use a mint, breath freshener or chew on some parsley, a natural breath freshener.

"It's showtime . . ."

In the movie, "History is Made at Night," the head waiter gathers the service staff for an inspection. He checks that their nails and hands are clean, their shoes are shined and their ties are straight. Then he goes over the night's specials. Today, this is still done in fine dining restaurants ~ so be prepared!

Wash and style your hair before your shift - Hair should be short or off of the neck. It must be constrained. Servers with long hair should use several hair ties – one close to the scalp and one or two throughout the length of the pony tail. It's advisable for female servers to wear their long hair up. There's nothing worse to guests than getting hair in their food. It ruins their appetites and, in many cases, they'll choose not to eat at all.

Take care of your hands - Guests will notice the condition of your hands, trust me. They'll see them every time you set a plate in front of them. You should try to keep your hands free from cuts, scratches and abrasions. If you do work outside of the restaurant that's rough on your hands, consider wearing gloves when doing these activities.

Your fingernails should be kept short and manicured. They need to be free from dirt and grease underneath. A guest who sees grime under a server's fingernails has to wonder what the *cook's* hands look like!

If you're going to wear nail polish, it should be clear or a very light shade. Dark red, black, brown, purple or green nail polish on a server is not attractive, appetizing or appropriate.

Wear a moderate amount of make-up - As little as you can feel comfortable with. There's a big difference between the make-up you'd wear on a date and what you should wear as a server.

Go light on scents - If you're going to wear a perfume or aftershave, make sure it's a mild scent. One of the joys of dining is the aromas of the food. You don't want to interfere with these delicate perceptions by wearing an overpowering scent.

Be conservative with jewelry - One small ring and a watch are appropriate. A watch is handy so that you can easily keep track of the timing of a table. Don't wear large bracelets or ornamental watchbands – any little crevice in them is a great breeding ground for bacteria.

Wear one or two earrings only; no nose, tongue or other facial rings. Guests will always be wondering when you last fiddled with one of these on your face – grossly unappetizing and inappropriate! Many restaurants ask that the male servers remove earrings while working a shift.

Groom facial hair - Male servers should always be clean shaven. A "five o'clock shadow" may look great in the movies, but not in a restaurant. Mustaches are generally acceptable when kept neat and trimmed. They should not extend below the mouth. Depending on the restaurant, well-trimmed beards are sometimes acceptable. Each restaurant has its own policies on these matters.

Wear an appropriate uniform - Make sure that you know the restaurant's policies regarding uniforms, and adhere to them. Uniforms should always be clean and pressed. A fresh shirt should be worn for each shift. When shirts become worn at the cuffs and collar, they need to be replaced. Shoes need to be clean and polished regularly. A typical server's uniform in an upscale restaurant is "black & whites" – a white tuxedo shirt, black pants (or skirt – remember your pantyhose, ladies!), black bow tie, black cummerbund, black shoes and black socks. At more casual restaurants, uniforms might include aprons, dress or polo shirts and khaki or black pants or jeans. Whatever the uniform code, be sure your clothing is neat and clean.

The need for good hygiene and a well-kept appearance is the same no matter what restaurant you work in. As you'll see, though, the styles of service can vary greatly . . .

Chapter 7

Getting food from kitchen to guest:
types and methods of service

There are a variety of service styles employed by different restaurants at different times. The same restaurant may use one style at breakfast or lunch and another at dinner. In this chapter, we'll touch on the most common styles of service that you might encounter during your career.

American Service - sometimes called "Plate Service" or "À la Carte Service". In this style of service, the server takes the order from the guests and delivers what's called the "dupe" to the kitchen. Traditionally, this was the top, soft copy or copies of the guest check, but today, most restaurants use some sort of POS (Point of Sale) computer terminal that will print out copies of the order at the various stations in the kitchen.

The guest decides how many courses he desires and orders from a menu on which items are individually priced. When the food is ready in the kitchen, the server delivers the food to the guest. This may be done either by using a banquet tray, cart or hand delivery.

If your restaurant's policy is to use banquet trays to transport food from the kitchen to dining room, the tray should be placed on a tray jack (a folding apparatus onto which a banquet tray is set) before serving. You should never hold the banquet tray and serve directly from it.

This style of service is probably the most common in the U.S. and is used at all levels – from casual family restaurants to some fine dining rooms.

Advantages of this style of service – It's relatively quick. No specialized service equipment is required. It's very personal – every guest has the individual attention of the server (or should have). It's easily taught and inexperienced servers can pick it up quickly.

Disadvantages of this style of service – It's labor-intensive. Stations have to be kept small. There's no way to maintain uniformity of service throughout the restaurant since some servers work faster and more efficiently than others.

Banquet Service - This type of service is used for a large group or groups. Generally, the menu is set for the entire party, though most restaurants will accommodate a request for a vegetarian option. The food is fully prepared and plated in the kitchen. It's then brought to the table on banquet trays and served from tray jacks. Service is usually done with a front waiter and a back waiter. The back waiter delivers the tray of food onto the tray jack and returns to the kitchen for another. The front waiter serves the food from the tray jack to the guest.

My preferred method of doing banquet service is to have specific waiters assigned to the tray-carrying detail. Other servers are assigned to place the plates in front of the guests. Still other servers take and deliver beverage orders and clear plates in a designated station. Service is done in an "S" or snake pattern in which one table is completed – then on to the next, until everyone is served *(see illustration below)*. Every guest should be on the same course at the same time.

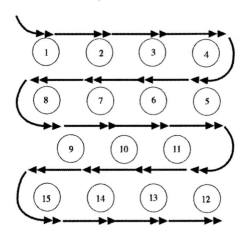

Banquet service done in an "S" or snake pattern

In Chapter 8, we'll cover the details of how to load, carry, unload and serve, using a banquet tray.

Advantages of this style of service – It provides rapid service for large groups of guests. A preset menu ensures that the kitchen prepares only what's needed. It takes fewer staff to serve a banquet

– there's no need to take menu orders.

Disadvantages of this style of service – It requires a large facility. It's a less personalized service, with less interaction between servers and guests. For the diner, there are fewer food options.

Buffet Service – This is generally a "help yourself" style of service. Plates and containers of food are arranged attractively on tables or carts. Sometimes a staff member is stationed behind the buffet line to assist the guests. Servers may take beverage orders, clear plates and replenish the buffet. Other server responsibilities can include maintaining the attractiveness of the buffet, cleaning up spills, keeping foods at appropriate temperatures (hot foods hot, cold foods cold) and describing dishes to guests.

Advantages of this style of service – It provides rapid service. It's easy to turn tables, (reuse the table for another seating). Only a small staff is required to service and maintain a buffet. It gives the

> **There's logic to that buffet layout . . .**
>
> *Did you ever notice how, on a buffet, all of the "good stuff" ~ the shrimp and smoked salmon, for example ~ is difficult to get to? This isn't by chance, but by design. All of the inexpensive product is placed at the beginning of the buffet. The restaurateur hopes you'll fill up on that! The more expensive foods are placed at the end and sometimes elevated to make it even more of a challenge to get to them.*

kitchen the opportunity to display artistic and creative skills. It also allows the kitchen to utilize leftovers. Guests like the chance to sample a variety of foods.

Disadvantages of this style of service – It requires a large facility. It's a less personalized service, with very little interaction between servers and guests. Portion control is now in the hands of the guest. There's often a lot of waste. A certain volume of business is necessary to make a buffet feasible.

Russian Service - Sometimes called "Platter Service". This is a team service concept. The team is usually composed of front waiter, back waiter and busperson. I have, on rare occasions, seen this service done with a single waiter and a busser. On the other hand, I've captained a team with seven members!

This is one of the most formal and elegant of services. The front waiter introduces and describes the menu to the guests and takes the order. The back waiter delivers the dupe to the kitchen or places the order through the POS terminal.

The food is fully prepared in the kitchen. It's artistically presented on heavyweight silver platters. Food is delivered tableside, either by using a tray and tray jack or, more commonly, by using a rolling cart.

The tray is presented to the guests for them to see the food before it's plated. Hopefully, at this point you'll hear some "oohs" and "aahs". The back waiter then places hot plates in front of the guests from the guest's right side. He continues to place plates while moving clockwise around the table. The captain will then offer the guests food from the silver platter. Generally, one platter will contain the meats and the other, offered subsequently by the back waiter, vegetable and starch (potatoes, rice, etc.).

The server stands to the left of the guest, holds the platter in his left hand, resting it on his forearm. He holds a serving spoon and fork in his right hand. The serving spoon and fork are then used the way you would tongs, (*yes, this does take practice!*) to serve the guest's choice from the platter. The spoon should be the utensil closest to the platter and is used to scoop up sauce or pan drippings. The back waiter completes the plate by offering the vegetables and starch. Service continues counterclockwise around the table, finishing with the host.

Using a fork and spoon to serve a guest

It's very important that the plate looks as attractive as if it had been assembled in the kitchen. Avoid spills. Be aware of the placement of the items on the plate. Each plate should look the same. Using an imaginary clock at each setting, place the protein at 6:00, the starch at 10:00, the vegetable at 2:00, or however management has deemed appropriate. Be artistic – coordinate the various colors of the foods and garnishes on the plate.

Advantages of this style of service – It's very elegant and sophisticated, with good customer/server interaction. Portions can be controlled. Russian Service is common at State dinners and, very often, a form of it is used on cruise ships.

Disadvantages of this style of service - Servers must be professional and experienced. There's a large outlay of monies for the serving equipment – silver platters, heavyweight serving utensils and attractive wooden rolling carts.

This may be a good time to get this "clockwise" and "counterclockwise" business cleared up. Does it really matter? Not really. Let me try to explain the logic behind it. Basically, you don't want to be moving backwards. This causes a number of problems, most important of which is you can't see where you're going and you can end up bumping into guests or fellow servers. When you're placing plates from the guest's right side using your right hand, you should continue service by moving clockwise. The procedure is the same when doing coffee service or clearing dishes, both done from the guest's right side. When you're serving from the left side of the guest, you continue service by moving counterclockwise. This way, you're always moving forward.

French Service - Sometimes called "Tableside Service". This, too, is a team service concept. The team is usually composed of front waiter, back waiter and busperson.

Like Russian service, this is a very formal and elegant type of service. The front waiter introduces and describes the menu to the guests and takes the order. The back waiter then places the order with the kitchen.

The food is *partially* prepared in the kitchen, then is completed tableside on a guéridon *(GARE-ee-DON)*, a cart that's equipped with a burner(s) or rechaud, *(rey - SHOW)* to keep the food hot.

The front waiter places the guéridon flush to the table, ready for service. When the food is delivered, he offers the platters to the guests for viewing. The plates are finished at the guéridon. Some examples of typical tableside preparation are:

- Salad dressings are made (Caesar, Wilted Spinach) and then the salads are tossed
- Steak Diane or Shrimp Scampi are fully prepared (meat or seafood is sautéed, sauce made)
- Chateaubriand or rack of lamb is carved
- Duck is flambéed (flamed with alcohol)
- Fish, such as Dover Sole, are de-boned and reassembled
- Desserts such as Crêpes Suzette, Bananas Foster, Cherries Jubilee are prepared (ingredients sautéed, sauces made, finished by flambéing)

The servers work quickly so that the guests all receive their food at the proper temperature. The entrées are completed with sauce, starch, vegetable and garnish. Again, the plates have to look as attractive as if they had been sent out by the chefs in the kitchen. Direction of service is the same as in Russian Service.

The caviar caper of '78 ...

I was serving caviar, tableside, to a group of diners. I divided the fish eggs equally onto the six plates my back waiter had provided and artistically arranged the toast points and garnishes. Everything was going great until I looked up ~ there were seven people at the table. I redistributed the caviar, doing my best not to let the guests know of the error ~ but how embarrassing! Always count your guests before you start serving!

Advantages of this style of service – It's the ultimate in personal service. You can actually tailor the recipe to the individual guest's taste. For hundreds of years it was the preferred service of the French nobility. Terrific guest/server interaction. A great opportunity for showmanship. You may encounter this style of service, or a modified version, in five-star resort hotel fine dining rooms.

Disadvantages of this style of service – It's a slow service, making it very difficult to turn tables. It's hard to find experienced personnel. The front waiter has to be knowledgeable in cooking techniques, times and temperatures as well as proper use of seasonings. The equipment, especially the guéridons, is extremely expensive.

Now that you have a basic understanding of the *types* of service, it's time to learn the proper way to serve. Keep in mind that, once you pick up these basic skills, you can put them to use in any food service setting – from a family restaurant to a world-class dining room.

Chapter 8

At the convenience of the customer:
basic techniques of table service

There's nothing mystical or particularly difficult about serving in a restaurant. It's a learned skill. Once you've acquired the basics, I'm not going to tell you that you're a waiter. Becoming a good server takes several years for most people. Like any other skill, it takes practice. Don't let yourself get frustrated. Don't fret over the possibility of dropping food or spilling beverages. It's going to happen. Although no one likes to see accidents, especially the restaurant manager (or worse yet, the owner), they can't always be avoided. Anyone who's been in the business for any length of time and tells you that he's never dropped or spilled anything, is just not being truthful.

In this chapter, you'll read a lot about "lefts" and "rights". When you see this, left means the diner's left, right means the diner's right. You'll learn that certain functions are done from one side of the guest, or the other.

We serve at the convenience of the customer - We want to serve without interfering with guests' conversations or interactions. If, for example, you notice that a guest makes a lot of gestures with his right hand while speaking, work from his left side. If a guest has his arm around his dining partner, don't make them separate for your convenience – serve from whichever side is less disruptive. When you can use the following rules, though, do so.

Place all food items from the left side of the guest - Serve all food (appetizer, soup, salad, entrée, dessert) from the left side. There are those restaurateurs who treat soup as a beverage and, therefore, serve soup from the right, but they're in the minority.

Remove all food items from the right side of the guest - Pick up all used plates, silverware and glasses from the diner's right side.

Place and remove all beverages from the right side of the guest - There are two schools of thought on serving beverages:

> *Stationary method* – At some restaurants, servers are trained to pour water and refill iced tea by pouring directly to the glass, with the glass remaining on the table. If you're going to do beverage service this way, it's advisable to wrap a clean serviette (napkin) around the water pitcher. Pitchers tend to have condensation on the outside surface. You don't want to leave droplets on the table or on the guests. Another consideration is that by pouring directly to the glass, there's a chance the water will splash.

When doing hot beverage service, always use a serviette. Wrap a small portion around the coffee pot handle and place the rest of the napkin as a barrier between the pot and the guest. When doing hot tea service, always bring a fresh pot of hot water and fresh lemon when delivering refills.

Lift-and-replace method - In this method, the server lifts the glass away from the table, pours the beverage and returns the glass to its original placement on the table.

When doing hot beverage service, lift the mug away from the guest, pour and return. When using a cup and a saucer, always lift *both* the cup and the saucer, pour, then replace. The cup or mug handle should be placed at 4:00 on the imaginary clock.

I utilize one method or the other, depending on the level of the service in the restaurant and the skill level of the servers. The stationary method works best when you have a skilled staff and an upscale, elegant dining room. The lift-and-replace method works better when you're in an informal setting and have a relatively inexperienced staff.

"Hug" your guest - Use the left hand when working at the guest's left and right hand when working at the right side. This is not as arbitrary as it might seem. There are some very good reasons to do this.

When you approach the table to serve food, always look for the guest's left arm. Serve with your left hand. If the guest needs something else, he can tell you because you're facing him. If you deliver the food with your right hand from the left side, you're backhanding the plate to the guest. This is rude. Also, if the guest needs something, he literally has to tap you on the shoulder to get you to notice him. If you're carrying a second plate in your right hand, switch it to the left hand for service to the next guest.

The same reasoning holds true when clearing or doing beverage service for the guest. Always use your right hand when you're at the right side of the guest so that you're always facing him, prepared to answer questions or offer additional service. All beverage glasses and cups are set on the right side of the guest, so it only makes sense to do the service from the right side.

Place plates properly - Place each plate on the table with fingers underneath and your thumb on the edge of the rim. It seems like it would be a good idea to place the plates on the palm of your hands so that you wouldn't have to touch the plate at all. But, when you carry plates in this manner you can only carry two at a time. Even more importantly, there's no easy way to get the plate off of your palm and onto the table. Give it a try.

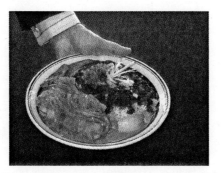

Place fingers under plate and thumb on the edge of the rim.

Most beginners think that a good server is one who can carry a lot of plates at one time. It's much more important that plates be carried *properly*. Food from one plate shouldn't end up on the bottom of another. Food shouldn't shift on the plate. When a plate is delivered, it should look the same as when it left the kitchen.

A plate should be set down in a position that will make it as attractive as possible to the guest. The main course should be placed so that the meat, fish or poultry (or the dominant part of the plate) is directly in front of the guest. To continue with the imaginary clock, this means that the protein should be placed at 6:00.

You should only carry as many plates as you're comfortable with. You don't want to appear as if you're juggling them. Never carry plates pressed against your body, struggling for balance. A professional server always wants to look graceful and under control.

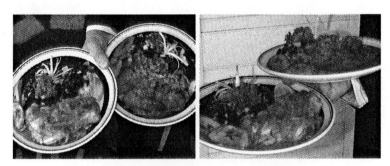

Both are correct ways to carry two plates

Try not to reach in front of a guest, or across one to serve another - The exception is when serving guests seated in a banquette (pronounced *bang KET* – a generally semi-circular booth). When serving guests in a booth, you'll find yourself saying, "Excuse me," often. If you have three people in a booth, no matter what you do, you'll always be crossing one of them to serve another.

Serve one guest at a time - Every guest should be made to feel like an individual. I watch servers all the time carrying a plate in each hand. They serve one plate to the guest on the left, using their left hand, and nearly simultaneously serve the guest on the right using the right hand. This is really lazy service. Serve one guest at a time. Move to the next guest, switch plates from right hand to left and serve.

Always use proper sanitation - Handle silverware, glassware and plateware hygienically. It doesn't matter whether you're setting, serving or clearing a table, always keep sanitation in mind.

Silverware should only be touched by the handles. Never handle a fork by its tines, a knife by its blade or a spoon by its bowl.

*Always handle silverware by the handle – **not** the tines, blade or bowl.*

Glassware should be held by the stem only, whether setting or clearing the table. Never have your fingers above the rim of the glass. Your fingers should be below what I call the "lip line", where guests lips have been, or will be. Don't place your fingers inside the rim of a glass. You don't want to pass your germs onto guests or be on the receiving end of theirs.

Plateware should be handled only by the rim. Never place fingers above or inside the rim of a coffee cup, mug or bouillon cup.

Never *have your fingers above the rim of a glass*   **Don't** *place fingers in a glass*   **Always** *hold stemmed glasses by the stem; others low on the glass*

When we're in the kitchen or side stations, we often handle food with our hands: removing rolls from the bread warmer; placing garnish on a plate or a lemon on the edge of an iced tea glass. You should never, though, allow a guest to observe you touching their food. In some restaurants, rolls are served by the staff from a bread plate or basket. I had a server offer rolls to a guest, then place it on the guest's bread plate with his *fingers*! Always use tongs or a pair of forks, in the French manner, to assist the guest. You may, as an option, ask the guest to please help himself as you hold the basket for him.

Use underliners - Always place any plate or bowl containing liquid or semi-liquid food on an underliner. An underliner is an appropriately sized plate with a doily. It serves a number of purposes. In this case, it keeps any spills off of the customer, yourself and the floor, where someone might slip on it. The most common underliners are saucers and bread plates. Items to be

The Main Course on Table Service

underlined include: soup in a bouillon cup, creamers, goosenecks, (what we might call gravy boats in our homes, generally used for serving sauces or gravy on-the-side), ramekins, (small, straight-sided containers used mainly for condiments) and monkey dishes (you learned what these are in Chapter 3). In some restaurants, iced teas and iced coffees are served with underliners. *When in doubt ... underline.* Each restaurant will have its own policy for the use of underliners.

Use a beverage tray - Always use a hand tray (also called a bar tray) when serving beverages. The tray is, in essence, your underliner. In case you spill some liquid, it will fall onto the tray not onto the floor, a guest or you. *Use a tray even if you're carrying only one glass.* When working a counter, there's no need to use a tray because, generally, there's only a small space and a small turn between the fountain and the counter.

Carrying beverages on a tray is the scariest part of the job for a beginning server. No one wants to spill water, a soft drink, or worse yet, a glass of wine onto a guest. Carrying a hand tray really isn't that difficult. It does, however, take practice.

Find the center of gravity of the tray. On an empty tray, it would be directly in the center. Spread your fingers out across the bottom of the tray. Every time you add something to the tray or take something off, you change the center of gravity.

The proper way to carry a hand tray

Don't load the tray while it's in your hand. Load beverages onto a tray in the kitchen or at the fountain on a steady, flat surface. Place the tray on your tray-carrying hand. It's best to carry a tray with your left hand, so you can serve the drinks with your right hand, which is the technically correct method. Still, I tell my servers to use whichever hand they are most confident with.

As a beginner, it's best to cluster all glasses in the middle of the tray. It'll be easier to balance the tray than if the glasses were on the perimeter. Leave room between the glasses so you can grasp them with your fingers. Slide the tray off of the counter, onto your hand. Use your other hand to help you find the center of gravity. When you feel balanced, let go with the helping hand. Walk, and don't look at your tray! That really *is* the secret – *don't* look at your tray! If you do, the liquid will start to move.

When you arrive at the table, place the opposite leg from the hand in which you're carrying the tray close to the table. If, for example, you're carrying a tray with your left hand, place your right leg close to the table. If you're tall, bend your knees a little when you place the glass to the right side of the guest's setting. Before you continue serving clockwise around the table, adjust your tray so that it's balanced again. This usually takes a small rotation of the tray in the direction from which the last glass was removed. Do this every time you remove a glass.

Want to keep that soup from sloshing? Don't look at it!

This phenomenon was explained by Marilyn Vos Savant in her "Ask Marilyn" column: "When you walk, you keep your balance smooth by orienting to your surroundings. If, instead, you orient to a bowl of soup you're carrying, you're orienting to a moving target . . . yourself!"

Some servers feel comfortable without making this tray adjustment. Do whatever works best for you.

Carrying a banquet tray - If you can carry a large oval tray, you can always find a job in the restaurant business. It isn't difficult. Here are the basics . . .

It's important that food gets to the guest at the proper temperature; hot foods hot and cold foods cold. Food must arrive and be presented to the guest looking attractive with no spilled soup on the underliner and no sauce or drips on the edges of plates. The food should be as attractively arranged on the plate as when it left the kitchen.

There's more "play" in a tray of food than in a tray of beverages. Food is generally solid, except for soups and some sauces, so it's possible to tilt the tray slightly without drastically affecting the placement of food on the plates.

Loading a banquet tray - Most operations that serve large parties use banquet trays and tray jacks. Often, plate covers are used, creating a base on which other plates can be stacked. When stacked, many more plates can be carried safely.

First, make sure that the tray is clean, top and bottom. Unless the tray has a non-skid surface of cork or other similar material, place a damp napkin on the inside of the tray to prevent articles from sliding. Load utensils and cold items before hot items. Load larger, heavier pieces toward the center of the tray; smaller pieces toward the edges. When using plate covers, stack cold food on top of cold food and hot food on top of hot food.

Don't place soup cups or goosenecks on underliners while on the tray. Stack all underliners separately. (*A helpful hint:* Place the doily from the top underliner beneath it or, by the time you get to the table, it will probably have blown off.) Balance the tray. Keep uncovered dishes away from the side of the tray that's nearest your hair. Have a tray jack ready to receive the tray. Leave one hand free to open doors and to clear a path, if necessary.

Lifting a banquet tray - Since a tray fully loaded with covered dishes can weigh more than fifty pounds, it must be lifted properly to avoid injury. There are advantages to carrying a tray on the left hand. Most kitchen doors are hinged on the right side. If you carry a tray on your right hand, the door is likely to swing back and hit your tray, jarring the food and causing plates to fall off. Having said that, carry the tray with whichever hand you're most confident.

Begin lifting the tray with your fingers facing front. As you lift, rotate your wrist so that, when the tray reaches your shoulder, fingers are facing back.

Make sure the tray is loaded properly. Check that the plate covers are on securely. Place the tray so that one long side of the oval extends several inches off the shelf or table from which you're picking it up. Grip the tray, on the short end of the oval, with your non-tray-carrying hand. Slide your tray-carrying hand under the tray at the center of the side on which the tray overhangs the shelf or table. Bend your knees and keep your back straight. As you lift, slide your tray-carrying hand to the point you've determined as the center of gravity of the tray. Stand, using your thigh muscles to do the lifting. As you stand, rotate the tray so that the tips of your fingers are turned toward your back. Slide the tray to your shoulder. This will feel awkward at the beginning.

Carrying and unloading a banquet tray - Hold and carry the tray above your shoulder, on the flat of the palm of your hand. Experienced servers will carry a tray on their fingertips. When you carry a tray this way, your fingertips act as "shock absorbers". The tray will "bounce" less.

If the tray is heavy, steady it with your helping hand and/or by resting it on your shoulder. Lower the tray the same way that it was lifted – by bending your knees and keeping your back straight. Steady the tray with your helping hand. Slide or place the tray onto the tray jack.

Unload plates from the center or alternate from opposite sides, keeping the tray balanced at all times. If the plates are unloaded from one side only, the tray will tip over. When you hear loud crashes in a dining room, this is usually the cause.

Always remove the plate cover before presenting the plate to the guest. When using a banquet tray, always use a tray jack. Never serve a guest directly from a banquet tray that's held in your hand.

Order of service - Simply put, a table is served in the following order: women first, from oldest to youngest (as you can imagine, this can test your tactfulness!), children, men and, finally, the host. Yes, the host gets served last. A good host wants to be sure that his guests are taken care of before he's served.

Clear when everyone is finished - In all but the most casual settings, wait until *everyone* at an individual table is finished before you start to clear. It's only polite to the slower diners in the party. When a server clears a table of dishes and one person is still eating, that person feels rushed and self-conscious. In Chapter 12, we'll discuss, in more detail, the correct procedures for clearing a table.

Now that you're familiar with how to serve a meal, let's get into the techniques of taking, placing and picking up the order . . .

Chapter 9

"Have you decided?"
taking, placing and picking up the order

Taking the order

Determine if the guests are ready to order. Try to decide if the party has a host or hostess (sometimes the dining room host/hostess will indicate this; sometimes one of the guests will ask to be presented with the check). I then always ask him or her if there are any time constraints on the party or if they're at leisure. Often, dinner is the entertainment for the evening, but sometimes the guests may be on their way to the theater or some other event and have to complete their meal by a particular time.

Most of the time you have to "read" the body language of the guests. Have they closed their menus and set them down on the table? Are they looking around for a server? If so, this is your cue that they're ready to order.

Know your station and your table numbers. If you use guest checks, have the top of them filled out with the table number, how many guests, your name (or initials), and the date. In many restaurants, especially those using a POS system, servers take the order on note pads, foregoing guest checks altogether.

Know your menu and your daily specials. When I ask a server about the daily specials and the reply is, "Let me check," the meal starts off on a bad note. Be able to pronounce menu items correctly and describe them concisely, yet appetizingly. Be aware of cooking techniques, cooking times, sauces and seasonings.

Know what's available – and what's not. It can really annoy a diner when he's spent ten minutes looking at the menu, only to be told, "We're out of that." In restaurant terms, this is known as "86"-ing an item. It's gone, so don't take an order for it. In my understanding, this comes from the bar side of the business. When it became obvious that a customer had too much to drink, the bartender was told to "86" him, which meant cutting the proof of the liquor down from 100 to 86. Since, often, these bar patrons also became rowdy, "86" soon meant tossing them out of the bar. The term was picked up by chefs to indicate when an item could no longer be offered to guests. Most kitchens will have an "86" board to let you know what they're out of. Sometimes it'll include a time when the item can be sold again ("Spaghetti – 15 minutes"). The board may also indicate how many servings of a particular item are still available. (When you sell an order, be sure to reduce the number). Check often, and make sure your guests are made aware if an item isn't available. Also communicate this information to your fellow servers.

When you're taking the order, give the guests your complete attention. Try not to be impatient (at least don't let it appear to the guests that you are). Don't glance anxiously around at the rest of your station.

Take every guest's order individually. One of my pet restaurant peeves is the server who stands at the head of the table and insists on taking every order without moving from his spot. While he's doing this, he makes himself the center of attention. All conversation at the table comes to a halt. A good server, in my estimation, is always unobtrusive and discreet.

That's no "guy" . . . she's my wife!

"Hi, how are you guys?" "What can I get you guys?" Every time my wife and I hear that in a restaurant, we cringe. Obviously, female guests aren't "guys," so don't refer to them that way. Instead, just use the collective word, "you," as in, "How are you?" "What can I get for you?" Your female guests will really appreciate this.

Stand erect, bending slightly forward from the hips. *Please*, no kneeling down to be at table height, leaning on the back of a chair, pulling a chair up to the table or plopping yourself down in the guests' booth to take the order. While some may find this a friendly approach, to most, it's an uncomfortable breach of the server/guest relationship. You're there to take their orders, not to be their "pal".

Begin taking the orders with a woman. Stand to her left and ask, "Have you decided?," "Are you ready to order?," or "May I take your order?" Try not to be stiff and formal, but do avoid slang or casual language. As mentioned in Chapter 5, "folks" is a little too informal a way to refer to your guests, but not nearly as bad as when a server asks female diners, "Are you *guys* ready to order?" Always use your best language and a natural tone. Speak with a "smile" in your voice.

Take the order clockwise around the table. Yes, you may notice that, when you're standing to the left of the guest, this means that you do have to move backwards, though I've said before that it's best not to do that. When we get to the subject of seat numbers, you'll understand the logic of this.

If possible, take all of the ladies' orders first. Then start back around and take all of the men's orders. Finish with the host. I'm always asked, "If the host is going to be doing the tipping, should I really serve him last?" Yes, you should. As mentioned earlier, a good host will always want to be sure that his guests' needs are taken care of before his own.

Be ready with your menu descriptions and recommendations. This is the time when guests will ask for suggestions or explanations of the menu items. Answer all questions briefly, though use wording that makes the dishes sound appetizing to the guests.

You'll need to work on your menu descriptions. Avoid generalities ("It's pretty." "It's tasty.") and slang ("awesome," "killer," "rad"). Terms like: fresh, light, delicate, tender, subtle, full-bodied and moderately spicy, are appropriate.

Don't allow your personal biases to enter into your descriptions or recommendations. If you don't eat meat, you can still recommend a meat entrée based on the feedback of other diners.

Do you hate to ask what a special costs? So do your guests.

They'll feel uncomfortable ~ and cheap. Unless your management specifies otherwise, tell your guests the price of the specials when you're describing them ~ ". . . and that sea bass special is $19.95" or "We have Clos du Bois Merlot on special this evening for $22.95 a bottle." I've been in many restaurants where the prices of specials are much higher than the menu prices. Diners deserve to know that. I've also known of restaurants where servers "float" prices, charging whatever they feel they can get away with. Now that's really unfair!

Making "winning" suggestions to a guest can help him to have a more enjoyable dining experience. It can also convert the guest into a "regular" – someone who will dine at the restaurant often. This is one of the best ways that I know of to create "call parties" – guests who ask to sit in your station when they return the restaurant.

Making recommendations to a guest doesn't necessarily mean suggesting the most expensive items on the menu. I think a lot of servers fall into this trap. As servers, we're in sales. We want to build our check and, subsequently, our gratuity. Guests know right away whether a server is sincere in his suggestions or is just thinking of his own wallet.

Find out what the guest is in the mood for. Try to determine his likes and dislikes. Would he prefer meat, fish or poultry? Is he an adventurous eater or is he more conservative in his dining habits? Does he have a good appetite or is he looking for something light? Suggest accordingly. It's a great advantage to be familiar with the food and to have tasted most of the menu items. Suggest those items that you especially like.

Repeat the order to the guest only to ensure accuracy. "You wanted the New York Steak, medium, with the sauce on the side?" Many service training manuals encourage the server to repeat every order back to each guest. I think this is overkill. Sometimes it becomes downright annoying. And, *please*, don't compliment the guest on what he orders ("Excellent choice!"). Would you tell him *not* to order a particular item? Telling a diner he's made a good choice implies that, if he'd chosen something else, it would have been a *poor* decision.

If you're in a restaurant that doesn't utilize a POS system, be sure that you're using the standardized abbreviations that have been set in place. Don't make up your own. If you use the proper abbreviations, you have a reasonable expectation of receiving the food that you ordered from the kitchen.

Now let's develop a system to accurately take the order and deliver it to the appropriate guest . . .

Let's call it the "seat designation system." It's also sometimes referred to as the pivot system. Most restaurants use some variation of this method.

Every table has a table number, so the kitchen and the servers know which table is to be served. Every seat at that table should also have a seat number. Some obvious focal point is decided on as the place where seat numbering starts. In my restaurants, the seat with its back to the front door is always seat number one. All seats are then numbered, continuing clockwise, around the table. Banquette seats are numbered from left to right. In bench-type booth seating, number as if the booth was a continuous semi-circle, as in a banquette (*see illustration below*).

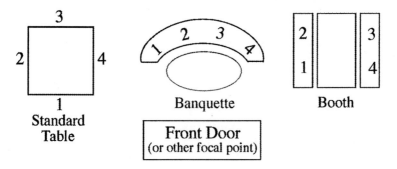

After taking each guest's order, make sure to indicate the seat number to the right of the abbreviation. Don't fill in the quantity column until all of the guests orders have been taken. Make note of all details (sauce on the side – abbreviated as "SOS" – etc.) and circle.

Take a "temperature" if necessary. What degree of doneness does the guest wish for his food? Temperatures are generally taken for beef and lamb. It's becoming more common to take a temperature for fish. The most common abbreviations for temperatures are:

R = Rare   *blue or cold in the center*

MR = Medium Rare   *red in the center*

M = Medium   *pink in the center*

MW = Medium Well   *fully cooked with no pink in center*

W(WD) = Well Done   *shoe leather*

Don't move on to the next guest until you're certain that you know exactly what the guest wants. A guest will never mind you rechecking his order to make sure that it's correct. No one wants to send food back to the kitchen because it's not what was ordered. The guest then ends up watching his tablemates eat while his order is being recooked. Most often, the reordered food arrives when the rest of the group is almost finished eating.

Circle all ladies' seat numbers and place an asterisk (*) next to the host's order. Remember, you may not be the person delivering the order. I've worked in restaurants where I never placed plates in front of the guests. It just wasn't part of my job.

Restaurant service really appears to be professional when food is delivered without an "auction". We all know what an auction is – you bid for a particular item and the highest bidder gets to purchase it.

In restaurant service, "auctioning" food is when a server, delivering food to the table, asks, "Who gets the hamburger?" You get the idea. If you use the seat designation system, no matter who delivers the food and beverages to the table, there should be no mistaking where they go. This isn't always as easy as it sounds. Sometimes as a server you'll be juggling several tables at a time, all at a different point in their meal.

Here's how your completed guest check might look:

Server	Table #	# Guests	Date
David	12	4	6/7/01

1	NY	(MR) (SOS) (2)	
2	Cod	1*, 3	
1	Hen	(4)	

Now you're ready to place your order in the kitchen.

Placing and picking up the order

The way you place an order will vary from one restaurant to another. Remember, you have already determined the time constraints, if any, on the guests. This will allow you to decide whether or not to immediately place the order with the kitchen.

Deliver the order to the kitchen. In team service, the front waiter will generally hand off the order to the back waiter for placement in the kitchen. The back waiter will deliver the dupes to the various stations. Most restaurants use guest checks with two dupes. One goes to the hot side of the kitchen, the other to the cold side.

In restaurants that use point of sale (POS) terminals, the back waiter will input the order. The printers at the two kitchen stations (hot and cold) will print out the orders.

Appetizers are usually "put up" (placed in the pick-up location for the servers) as they're ready. Entrées are generally partially prepared by the kitchen staff and then "fired" (finishing the preparation and/or cooking) at the server's request. This is done just before the previous course is cleared.

Ask for your order. The back waiter announces to the kitchen, "Pick up, please, table number 12." At this point, he'll collect all utensils, underliners and garnishes for his order.

Pick up cold foods first and place them on the tray or cart. Next, pick up hot foods and place them on the tray away from the cold foods. Cover the hot entrées with a plate cover, if your restaurant uses them. Check the appearance of the plates as you pick them up. Are they properly garnished? Or are you to garnish them? Make sure that the plate is clear of dripped food, fingerprints and smudges.

Compare your pick up order with what is written on your guest check. Does it match? If several steaks were ordered, do you know which one is the rare? Were special instructions followed by the kitchen? Is the sauce on the side (SOS) of the entrée, as it was ordered?

Deliver the food. Carry the tray, slowly roll the cart or hand-carry the plates into the dining room. Serve the food to the guests, as ordered. If possible, serve the ladies first. Don't auction off food unless you have no other option.

While you're taking orders from one table, the diners at the next may be just arriving and the ones on the other side may be ready to place a dessert order. Obviously, timing is extremely important in restaurant service. How do you achieve that delicate balance between rushing your guests and having them feel like they've been waiting forever for their meals? Let's find out . . .

Chapter 10

Taking the "wait" out of waiting tables:
sequence and timing of service

You'll find that the sequence of service varies from one property to another. In general, though, the points in the meal where timing is most critical are:

• Initial contact
• Service of first beverage
• Service of first course
• Check presentation

Host/hostess greeting – The host or hostess usually has the initial contact with the guest (you'll read more about the important duties of the host/hostess in Chapter 13). All guests should be acknowledged within thirty seconds of their arrival. They should be seated within a minute of the initial contact, or offered a place to wait until their table is ready. When seated, the host/hostess, in essence, turns the guests over to the servers' care.

Server greeting – Ideally, the server should be at the table when the host/hostess arrives, to assist in seating the guests. If you can't be there when the guests are being seated, make sure that a member of the service team greets the guests within one minute. Even if you can't begin service right away, acknowledge them in passing, and let them know that you'll be there in just a moment.

Many training manuals instruct servers to introduce themselves by name. I'm not fond of this practice. If the guest wants to know your name, he'll ask.

Beverage service and menu presentation - In many restaurants, the hostess will hand out the menus to the guests. Menus are always presented from the guest's left. If this is the case, the server should take a beverage order at this time. Production and delivery of the beverage should be done quickly; within three minutes.

Once he's served the beverages, the server should offer the specials of the day. He might also offer to further explain menu items or, if the guests seem interested, offer a few suggestions.

In most upscale restaurants, the server will take the beverage order and deliver the drinks *before* he presents menus. Some restaurants have a policy that menus shouldn't be presented until the guests have ordered (or declined) a second round of drinks, or a wine list has been requested. Then, the server asks the host if he'd like to have menus presented. "May I leave menus with you at this time?" or "Would you like to see menus now?" This would be the appropriate time for the server to offer the daily specials.

Food order is taken - This is one of those times when you have to "read" the table. If, through body language, the guests appear to be ready, proceed. In an upscale restaurant, I always ask the host if I may begin to take the orders. Don't just walk away from the guest after taking his order – always thank guests individually.

Bread and butter service - Bread and butter is traditionally served at this time. Many restaurants have a community butter plate that's placed in the center of the table, along with a basket of rolls or bread. In upscale restaurants, the busser will offer rolls and butter to the guest, from the guest's left side, using two forks to deliver them to the bread and butter plate. Follow restaurant guidelines and guests' preferences here. Generally, we serve one pat of butter and one roll to each guest.

Delivery of food - The first course (appetizer, soup or salad) must be delivered quickly; within 10 minutes. Once guests have a beverage and a first course in front of them, they're comfortable for awhile and will settle into the rhythm of the meal.

Entrées should be delivered within 20 minutes if that's all the guest has ordered. Inform the guest as to approximately how long it should be until his entrée is served. Twenty minutes can seem like an eternity to a hungry diner, so make sure that bread and butter has been served.

When one or more courses are served before the main course, entrées should be delivered within 10 minutes after the preceding course has been cleared.

Check back – Once guests have had a chance to taste their food, give them two minutes and check back to see if they're happy with their choices.   Make sure that they've had enough time to actually

"How's your meal?"
"Vwrgdsuhfrr."

Excuse me? "Very good so far," your guest repeats once he's had a chance to swallow. Servers always seem to catch diners in mid-bite. In fact, it happens so often, a guest has to wonder if it's intentional. Sometimes it is. In private, servers will admit to doing this as a way to amuse themselves. Guests rarely find it so funny. Give diners a chance to swallow before you do your "check back." They'll appreciate it.

taste their food! Some appropriate verbiage: "Is everyone enjoying dinner?" or "Is everything to your satisfaction?" Don't say, "Is everything OK?" A restaurant should always strive to be better than "OK". Okay indicates that things might be acceptable, but not particularly good. If a guest appears to be dissatisfied, offer to exchange his dish. (More on this in Chapter 17).

Dessert - After completely clearing and crumbing (sweeping crumbs from the table), it's time to offer desserts. Many restaurants have separate dessert menus. Present these as you would any menu, from the guest's left side, opened and ready for the guest's perusal. *Make sure the menu isn't upside down!* If the dessert options are to be presented orally, or you'll be showing guests desserts on a tray or cart, do so at this time. Again, make them sound irresistible.

Coffee or tea should be offered and coordinated with the dessert service. Desserts should be delivered within 10 minutes of the entrée plates being cleared, or the dessert order being placed.

Some desserts, such as soufflés, have a long preparation time. These items should be suggested to the guest when taking the initial dinner order. A soufflé can take 45 minutes to prepare. They're also very unstable, so when they're ready, they have to be served immediately or they'll "fall" and the presentation will suffer.

Table maintenance - You should continuously bus the table. Empty drink glasses and bottles should be removed. Always ask, "May I?" and wait for the guest to answer – he may not be quite ready to give up that last sip of Scotch. Place a clean napkin over any spills. Remove all unnecessary silverware, condiments and paper scraps (like opened sugar packets), beverage napkins and straws.

Pacing - There should be no long gaps between courses. There's a delicate balance here – you don't ever want the guest to feel rushed, but a guest also shouldn't sit without food in from of him for more than 10 minutes. Again, it's a matter of being able to read a table.

Check presentation - The check should be presented within seconds of the guest's request. The server should anticipate the presentation of the bill and have it ready. Once more, it's necessary to read the table. When it's apparent to you that there's nothing else that the guests desire, present the check.

Who gets the check? If it's obvious that there's a host of the party, he or she gets it. When you're not sure, place the check at the center of the table (or in a neutral position) and let the guests work it out. If they're really arguing over who's picking up the tab, the rule is that the person under whose name the reservation is made is considered the host.

In the finest restaurants, it's appropriate to present the check only when the host requests it.

Place the check in a sleeve, or total-side down on a doilied plate, and present to the guest. In a casual restaurant, it may be the policy for the guest to take the check to the cashier, at the front of the restaurant, to be settled. In most upscale restaurants, the server will service the check. Inform the guest that you'll handle the check for him: "Whenever you're ready, I'll take that for you," or "I'll take that whenever you're ready."

Always remain visible throughout the meal – but even more so at the close of it. Let me stress again the importance of your timing here. When the guest is ready to leave, he's ready to leave. He doesn't want to have to hunt down his server. Even if you've done everything perfectly throughout the meal, but you mess up the timing of the check presentation, that's what the guest will remember. It can ruin his perception of his overall dining experience – and be reflected in your tip.

Servicing the check - If the transaction is to be completed with a credit card, service it through the data capture machine. This is a device that will transmit data back and forth between the restaurant and the credit card company. You'll be given an approval code. Return the check and the credit card voucher promptly to the guest. Provide a pen for the guest's use. When the guest has signed and completed the credit card voucher, be prepared to remove the guest's copy and give it to him.

"Here's your card, Ms. Rothschild" . . .

Those are the magic words that earn servers an extra bonus from my wife. When we're dining out and she pays with her credit card, we eagerly wait to see what the server will do when he or she returns with the credit card and voucher. If it's placed directly in front of Barbara or, even better, handed to her with "Thank you, Ms. Rothschild," they've taken the time to check the name on the card and will be rewarded with an extra tip. Why not add this personal touch to your service? Who knows? Maybe you'll get a bonus, too!

Never assume that the man at the table is the host. If a credit card has been placed in a check sleeve, look at the name. If the credit card belongs to a woman, return it to her for her signature. Again, it may be difficult to determine exactly which guest is paying. In that case, it's safest to return the check sleeve containing the credit card and voucher to the center of the table.

If it's a cash transaction, make change in such a way as to give the guest a variety of tipping options. Never ask, "Do you need change?" This makes it look like you expect the guest to leave the change as a tip. Return all cash change to the guest, unless he's told you to "keep the change" or "the rest is for you."

Thank You - As the guests are organizing to leave the restaurant, be sure to thank them. "Thank you for dining with us," "It was a pleasure to serve you," are appropriate parting comments. You might also offer to help guests with their coats, if they have them at the table. Make sure that you say good night to each and every guest on the way out. Extend an invitation for the guest to return: "We hope you've enjoyed everything and will be back soon."

Reset the table - Place a high priority on clearing the table and resetting, especially when it's very busy. The manager and hostess may have guests breathing down their necks for a table. At the end of the shift, it may be the restaurant's policy to stop resetting tables. Some restaurants use tablecloths for the evening service, placemats for breakfast and lunch.

In the paragraph above, I mention *resetting* the table. It may occur to you that so far I haven't taught you how to *set* a table. Why wait until this point in the book to talk about that? Because until you understand the basics of service and *why* things are placed where they are, setting the table won't make as much sense. Now, though, it should. So let's get into the proper way to set a table . . .

Chapter 11

"Where do I put the fish fork?":
preparing the side station and setting the table

When entering a restaurant, a guest will make his first judgement: Am I going to like this restaurant, or not? One of the things a guest will subconsciously notice, because it makes him feel comfortable, is a sense of symmetry, or balance, throughout the room. The tables should be evenly spaced, one from another. Each should be set exactly like the one next to it.

Side work and side stations

Before the server can begin setting the tables, some other duties need to be performed. These activities are part of what we refer to as *side work*.

Specific tasks that need to be done to prepare for table setting include:

- Polish silverware and glassware to remove any water spots or smudges
- Fold napkins
- Fill salt and pepper shakers and sugar containers
- "Marry" condiments if they're part of your table setting (this means combining partial bottles to be sure that each bottle that's placed on the table is full)

- Check floral arrangements to be sure they're fresh and attractive
- Check that all table tents and other tabletop items are clean and in good condition

In addition to making sure that all items are ready for table setting, you may be responsible for stocking and setting up your *side station*. Someone needs to do this before, during and after each shift. This is a server's work and prep area where the items that are commonly used during the meal are kept. It's extremely important that you keep your side station clean, neat and well-stocked. It'll save you valuable time and steps during busy service periods. Here are some of the items that can typically be found in a server side station:

- Hotplates with coffee and hot water
- Thermal serving carafes
- Tea bags
- Hot tea set-ups (individual tea pots and underliners)
- Cups and saucers, if they're not part of the table setting, or mugs
- Water pitchers with iced water
- Iced tea pitchers
- Ice and ice scoops
- Lemon wedges or slices
- Individual butter pats
- Filled creamers and extra containers of cream and milk
- Salt, pepper and sugar for refilling tabletop containers

- Condiments – mustard, ketchup, hot sauce, steak sauce
- Wrapped straws
- Beverage napkins
- Doilied plates to be used as underliners
- Tablecloths and folded napkins
- Additional polished silverware and glasses for resets (including iced tea spoons)
- Wine buckets

Other duties that can fall into the category of side work may include:

- Preparing garnishes for food and beverage items (sometimes includes slicing lemons and limes, making bundles of herbs for plate garnishes)

- Checking the restrooms to be sure they're clean and well-stocked

- Cleaning windows, mirrors, etc.

- Vacuuming/sweeping/dusting (yes, servers are sometimes asked to do these chores!)

- Shaking linen – emptying out the linen bin, placing a cloth on the floor and shaking out all debris from the other soiled cloths to be sure no silverware, etc. is being discarded, then bundling up all the linen and placing it for pickup.

Setting the table

Great care must go into each setting. It's important to set each restaurant table as you would for guests at your home. When tables are carelessly set, the guests may also become concerned about what kind of care goes into the preparation of the food in the kitchen.

The first step in setting the table is to make sure that all of the tables and chairs are stable. If a table is unsteady, use the adjustments on the bottom of the table legs or base to level it. If necessary, use a small wedge of cardboard or a matchbook to keep the tabletop from moving. If you find a wobbly chair, replace it with one that's more stable. When a guest sits down at a table with an unsteady top or chair, he, too, is going to feel off-kilter. This is *not* a good start to his dining experience.

Here are suggested steps in table setting:

Get instructions from your manager - Determine what the table arrangements are to be in your station for this shift:

- Do you need to pull out a table leaf to enlarge the table capacity or do you need to pull two tables together to accommodate a large party?
- How many seats are to be at each table?
- Is a special napkin fold to be used?
- Which pieces of flatware are required?

- What sort of plateware is to be preset?
- What glasses are to be preset?

Organize your station - Place the tables in the specified arrangement, with the proper number of chairs around. Seat #1 should be easily identifiable by anyone on the service team (remember, this is the seat with its back to the front door or whatever focal point your restaurant uses). Check to be sure that the seats are free of crumbs. Evenly space the chairs around the table. If there's an even number of seats, the chairs should be directly across from one another. With an odd number of chairs, there should be an equal amount of space between the chairs. To check the placement of the seats, stand behind a chair. In the case of a table with an even number of seats, you'll see a chair directly across from you. With an odd number of seats, you'll see an empty space across from you (a 16-year-old student showed me this trick). Do your best to avoid placing seats where guests will need to straddle a table leg. Keep in mind, too, that, once the cloth has been placed, the edge of the chair seat should just touch the tablecloth, so don't push the chairs too far under the table.

Place the tablecloth on the table - Be sure you have the right size tablecloth. A cloth should not extend below the seat of the chair. Make certain it's free of stains and is well ironed. Determine that the cloth is right side up. Most cloths have a sewn hem, just like your clothing. The rough edge of the hem is the bottom side of the cloth (sometimes it'll be easy to spot since there will be a manufacturer's tag!). If the cloth has been properly laundered, the top of the crease should be facing up, not down.

Center the cloth on the table. The cloth should be an equal distance from the floor on all sides. Generally, the center crease should be in the center of the table. In a booth, the crease should run across the center lengthwise.

Place centerpiece objects on the table - If flowers are used, place them first, directly in the center of the table. Next, place the salt, pepper and sugar. Always polish everything before it's set out on the table. Make sure that the salt and pepper shakers are filled to capacity and clean, not sticky to the touch. Most restaurants use sugar packets in a holder. This, too, should be completely filled, with no open packets. When a table is against a wall, the centerpiece objects should be placed close to the wall, centered on the width of the table.

Setting the cover - In restaurant language, "cover" has two meanings. It can be an individual guest, as in, "I had 20 covers in my station tonight." It also means an area directly in front of each guest of approximately 18-24 inches, which would encompass a complete setting. This includes china (plateware), cutlery (silverware), napery (in this case, napkins) and glassware.

The "set line" is an imaginary line about one inch from the edge of the table. Nothing should be set closer to the edge than this line.

The shape of the table doesn't matter. The reasoning is that anything set close to the edge of the table is likely to end up on the floor.

Determine which napkin fold is to be used. Place the napkin in the center of the cover, directly in the middle, lined up with the chair. The most common napkin fold is the "tent" or "pyramid". If the napkin fold has a point, the point should face toward the customer. (Having said that, I don't think I've ever been in a Chinese restaurant where the point of the tent fold didn't face *away* from the guest. I don't

> **Tip-top tabletops . . .**
>
> *When you set your tabletop items (salt & pepper, sugar, etc.) take a minute to make sure that any table tents or other printed materials that remain on the table are clean and in good shape. Servers, bussers and hostesses should also be sure that all menus presented to guests are free of fingerprints, smudges and food and that they're not worn. In this age of computer-generated printing, there's no excuse for presenting a shabby menu.*

know why this is. Maybe it has something to do with *feng shui*, the ancient Chinese art of placement that dictates you should never point a sharp edge at yourself or someone else?)

In a formal setting, a show plate will be the center of the cover. This is usually a decorative plate, sometimes with the restaurant's logo or artwork (*note:* be sure that the logo or design is facing the guest). The show plate (also called a trencher, charger, base plate, face plate, place plate and service plate) is meant as a placeholder for the courses that follow. Because the show plate is meant to be seen by the guest, you don't want to cover it, so the napkin is then set to the left of the forks, or specially folded and placed in a glass.

If this is a banquet setting, or if you have a party with a preset menu in your station, the menu dictates which pieces of silverware are required. Silverware is never set just to make the table look pretty. Only set those pieces that are required for the meal. It's always set in the order in which it's to be used, working from the outside of the cover toward the napkin or show plate. Otherwise, set your table according to restaurant policy.

Be sure that the silverware you're about to set out is all in good shape. There should be no tarnish. Fork tines should not be bent. Don't set out anything that you wouldn't eat or drink from.

All silverware must be polished before it's set out. Commercial dishwashers tend to leave water spots on plates, glasses and especially silverware. Take a *lightly* dampened cloth and polish out the water spots. Be careful not to leave streaks. Polish the entire piece of silverware – *including* the handles.

Silverware should be set out in neat, orderly rows. The bottoms of the individual pieces should be lined up. If the restaurant staggers forks (offsetting the ends of the fork handles slightly from each other), they should be done the same way on every table in the dining room.

Forks are placed to the left of the napkin or show plate with the tines facing up. In Europe, or European-style American restaurants, the tines face down because of the different eating method used and to showcase the monogram or other etching on the silver. Knives and spoons are placed to the right of the napkin or show plate. Knife blades should face toward the forks. Spoons should be placed on the table with bowls facing up (except in the European style, where the bowl would face down). Allow approximately 10-12 inches between the forks and the knife.

Keep the room looking great ~ even when you're closed . . .

You never know who's going to see your dining room, even when you're not there. Maybe a meeting planner is checking out the facilities for a big group. Or a potential guest stops by to get a feel for the restaurant's ambiance. Sometimes you won't be able to reset for the next shift (if the carpet needs to be shampooed or the exterminator is expected) but, whenever possible, be sure the dining room is fully set and looking its best.

Remember, at some point, an entrée-sized plate has to fit into that spot.

When replacing used silverware during service, always carry the clean silverware to the table on a small tray or a napkin-lined plate. Be careful not to get your fingerprints on them.

Glassware - If the dining room is set at the end of the shift to get ready for the next meal period, glasses should be set on the table upside down. This helps to keep them free from dust. Polish out the water spots. Some servers like to invert their glasses over steaming water, then polish out the spots.

The water glass, in most settings, is placed directly above the tip of the knife blade. A wine glass, if one is to be set, is placed to the right of, and below, the water glass. Glasses should only be handled by the stem or the base.

Plateware - If the restaurant table setting includes a bread and butter plate ("B&B" in restaurant terms), it's placed just above the forks. It may also be set to the left of the forks.

If a butter knife, or butter spreader is used, it should be placed on the bread and butter plate parallel with, and closely aligned to, the forks with the blade facing left. Some restaurants place the butter knife perpendicular to the forks, in the top third of the plate with the blade facing toward the guest.

If a cup and saucer are part of the cover, the cup should be placed on the saucer, bowl down, with the handle at an imaginary 4:00 position.

Now your tables are set and you're ready for service. But just as important as *setting* the table properly is *clearing* it properly. Here's how . . .

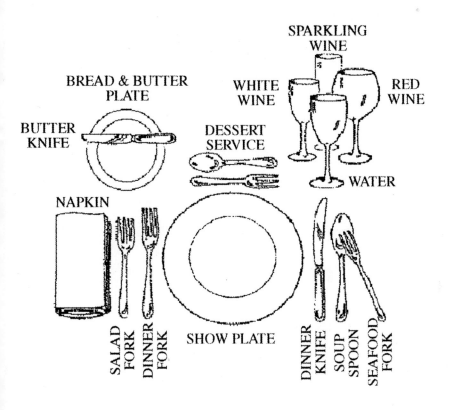

SPARKLING
WINE

BREAD & BUTTER
PLATE

WHITE
WINE

RED
WINE

BUTTER
KNIFE

DESSERT
SERVICE

WATER

NAPKIN

SALAD
FORK

DINNER
FORK

SHOW PLATE

DINNER
KNIFE

SOUP
SPOON

SEAFOOD
FORK

Formal Table Setting

Chapter 12

"May I take that for you?":
clearing the table

Clearing the table, or bussing, refers to the act of removing used silverware, plates and glasses when they're no longer in use. We've touched on some of this is Chapter 10, under table maintenance. Here, we'll look at it in more detail.

A table has to be bussed continuously. You never want it to start looking messy. All restaurant managers will tell you: "Never walk into the kitchen empty-handed." It just makes sense. Don't let things pile up. There's always something you can drop off at the dishwashing area on your way into the kitchen.

General rules – Wait until all of the diners have finished the course before removing soiled plates. The exception to this is when one of the guests is having more courses than the rest. Say, for instance, all of the guests are having soup, but one is also having salad. Clear his soup bowl and serve his salad, but leave the rest of the guests' soup bowls in front of them. When the guest is finished with his salad, remove all of the dishes.

Bus the plates when the guests have indicated, through body language, that they're finished. Another way to tell is by the placement of their silverware. When a guest lays down his knife and fork together on the right side of the plate, he's signaling that he's done eating. If a guest places his napkin on his plate (*yuk!*) or pushes the plate away from him, you should also clear his plate. When in doubt, ask, "May I take your plate?" or "Have you finished?" (Remember to wait for their answer before you take the plate.) Remove all plates from the right side of the guest, using your right hand. Don't stack plates on top of each other or scrape food from one to another in front of the guests.

When a course has been served on an underliner, as a cup of soup might be, remember to remove the underliner at the same time as the cup, in one smooth motion. When a show plate is preset on the table, remove it along with the dishes used for the previous course, before the entrée is served. Dinner plates are often similar in size to the show plate and it's awkward to set one on top of the other.

Move clockwise around the table. Don't juggle plates. You always want to look confident and in control. Remove only as many dishes as you're comfortable with at one time. Remember your sanitation. Pick up glasses only by the base or stem, utensils by the handle and plates by the rim.

Clear tables as quietly and as quickly as possible. Diners at other tables should be unaware of your activities.

Most restaurants have server side stations or bus stations. This is where you'll most often place your dirty dishes. A bus cart with plastic bus boxes is usually placed in the bus station. Neither the bus cart nor bus boxes should be brought to the table. The plates, glasses and flatware are always brought to the cart.

Scrape food from the plates into the trash. Separate and stack dishes according to size with small dishes on top of larger ones. Place glasses in a separate bus box. This helps to minimize breakage (and cut fingers) as well as making the cleaning process easier at the dishwashing area. Silverware is generally placed in a container that has a little pre-soaking solution.

When the bus cart is ready to be rolled into the kitchen, the bus boxes should be covered with a napkin so they're not quite as unsightly as they pass quickly through the dining room.

Some restaurants are set up so that you bus directly to the dishwasher area. In this case, you'll find yourself becoming an efficient busser quickly since you'll want to make as few trips as possible.

Some restaurants have you place your dirty plates on a tray and tray jack. Again, stack dishes according to size. Scrape the plates into the center of the tray. Place glasses solidly on to the tray. Never stack glasses one inside of another. Separate silverware to one side of the tray. *Never place dirty dishes on a tray with fresh food ready for service.*

While guests are at the table - Use a bar tray to save steps and time, especially when clearing glasses. The tray should not be

**Hey, that's not trash,
it's tomorrow's lunch!**
*Here's a lesson you can learn from
my mistake: I was clearing the table
of a family who were regular
guests. I'd already picked up some
of the plates when the daughter
asked to have the rest of her food
packed to take home. I said I'd take
care of it and continued clearing,
placing her plate above the rest.
When she saw what I'd done, she
said, angrily, "Well, now I don't
WANT to take it!" The moral of the
story: Never let it even APPEAR
that you're mixing trash and "to
go" food. One other helpful hint:
Never leave a plate sitting in the
kitchen that needs to be boxed up.
By the time you get back, I
guarantee a busser or another
server will have eaten it.*

placed on the table. When clearing the table just prior to dessert, clear a complete setting at a time: entrée plate, bread & butter plate, all silverware not necessary for dessert. The community butter plate and bread basket should also be removed. In the finest restaurants, the salt and pepper shakers are also removed since there's no need for them with dessert. Remove the crumbs from the table either with a crumber or with a folded napkin. Always sweep the crumbs onto a small plate, not onto the floor.

The only items that should remain on the table at this time are: water glass, unfinished beverages, dessert flatware and cup and saucer if they were part of the table setting.

Leftovers - Always offer to wrap unfinished food for the guest to take with them. Don't bring takeout boxes to the table and expect guests to pack up their own food – this is really unappetizing for other diners. Instead of calling the wrapped food a "doggie bag", let's call it "tomorrow's lunch" or something creative to indicate that this food is so good that they'll want to eat it again. Wrap it up neatly and securely, so that it won't leak.

When dessert is finished, clear the dessert plate and all of the remaining silverware. Offer to refill coffees.

When guests have vacated the table - When guests have all left the table and you're clearing, pick up all of one item before starting on another: glasses, plates, etc. You may, in this case, place your bar tray directly onto the table. Remove all dirty napkins, paper goods (opened sugar packets, dessert menus, etc.). Crumb the seats or banquettes, using a napkin. If your tabletop doesn't include a cloth and you need to wipe down the table, be sure to use different napkins for the tabletop and the seat. This is a very common complaint from restaurant guests – they don't want to see you use the same napkin to wipe a table after you've used it to wipe chairs.

Change the cloth and reset - When you're ready to change the tablecloth, always have a fresh cloth with you. The bare tabletop is often not very attractive, so try to leave it exposed for as short a period of time as possible. Tablecloths should not be waved in the air by the server to open them. It's distracting to diners at the adjacent tables. Keep the tablecloth flat on the table when spreading. With some practice, you'll be able to place a fresh cloth on the table without exposing the tabletop at all. Reset the table according to the manager's request.

At this point, your host or hostess is probably ready to seat another party at that table you've just reset and it's time to start the service procedures all over again. It's part of that host's or hostess' job to help keep the dining room organized and running smoothly. How do they do this? Let's find out . . .

Chapter 13

Greeting and seating:
how the host/hostess can set a positive tone for the meal

The guests' first contact is usually with a host or hostess, who greets them and then escorts them to a table. He or she makes the first impression on a guest – and first impressions count! This position is truly one of the most important in the entire restaurant. It should be filled with a competent and even-tempered individual.

From now on, I'll refer to this person as female, since a great percentage of those in this position are women.

Be sure to smile. Show the guests that they're important and you're glad they've chosen to dine at your restaurant. If the staff is well-groomed, efficient and makes a guest feel welcome; if the restaurant is clean and inviting; the guest's experience starts on a positive note.

Responsibilities

Taking reservations - In most restaurants, the hostess will take the reservations according to the directions of the Maître d' or Dining Room Manager who will generally create a template, setting a maximum number of people for a given time frame. For example, he may ask that reservations for no more than 20 people be taken at 7:00 PM, and a maximum of 15 at 7:30 PM.

This is the way the reservation sheet may look for that night when the hostess comes on shift.

Time	Guests' Name	# in party
7:00	Ross	4
	Alford	6
7:30	Caldwell	4
	Murphy	6

In this case, the hostess may take reservations for 10 more people at 7:00 PM and approximately five more at 7:30 PM. Once a time slot has been filled, the hostess should offer the next available time to the guest.

The manager sets up this system to ensure that the restaurant operates smoothly. Through his experience, he's learned how many diners the servers and the kitchen can handle at one time. Taking more reservations than the staff can handle would lead to an unpleasant dining experience for the guests.

It's also important to be aware of how long it takes to "turn" a table – the amount of time the guests will occupy the table before it can be reset and reused. In fine dining establishments, the general rule is to allow two hours before re-booking the table. This means that a table that has been seated at 7:00 can't be expected to turn until 9:00. In more casual restaurants, the turn can be completed in a little more than an hour.

Answering the phone - Most reservations are taken over the telephone. Here, the guest's first impression of the restaurant is through the person who answers the phone. Some restaurants have set scripts for what to say. It might be something like, "Good afternoon. Thank you for calling the Mayflower Restaurant. Becky speaking. How may I assist you?" Use the script every time you answer the phone. This ensures that every call is answered in the same courteous manner, no matter which staff member takes the call.

Answer all calls by the third ring - If the phone isn't answered promptly, the caller starts to wonder about the efficiency of the rest of the operation. The caller may also assume that the restaurant is too busy for someone to answer the phone, or that it may be closed, and might decide to take his business elsewhere.

Speak with a smile in your voice - Sound happy to hear from the caller. He's a potential customer. Allow the person to hear your genuine delight that he's called your restaurant. Never let him think, from your tone, that you're interrupting something more important to take his phone call.

Use your best vocabulary and manners - Avoid slang as you would in any other area of service. Speak in your normal voice. Don't use that "radio DJ" voice. Speak clearly and confidently.

Get accurate information - The basic information that you're seeking from the caller is: What date is the reservation for? At what time would you like the reservation? How many, total, in your party?

"Airheads" need not apply ...

Chris Sherman, food critic for the St. Petersburg (FL) Times, said that one of the things he looks for in restaurant service is a quick greeting at the door.

"If I have to stand there for five minutes, it's as aggravating as hell," said Sherman. "The hostess job is usually given to the most airheaded, least trained of the servers. It should be the opposite."

~ from Restaurants and Institutions, October 1, 1993

Some other possible questions to ask, depending on restaurant policy, are: "Would you prefer smoking or non-smoking?," "Are you celebrating a special occasion?" It's a good idea to repeat the information back to the guest, to ensure its accuracy.

Thank the guest - Always thank the guest for his call. If a reservation has been made, a statement such as "We look forward to seeing you then!," is appropriate. If the call was merely for informational purposes, a good sign-off might be, "We hope you'll decide to dine with us soon! Thank you for your call."

Greeting the guest when he arrives - Remember, you only get one chance to make a first impression! The salutation, or greeting, should be something like, "Good Evening. Welcome to the Mayflower Restaurant. How may I help you?"

Ask guests if they've made a reservation. Make all guests feel welcome, reservation or not. Most restaurants welcome walk-in business. Sometimes, of course, you won't be able to accommodate guests without a reservation, or at least not immediately. Those with reservations must have priority.

The guest with a reservation will usually announce himself, "I'm John Smith, and I have a 7:30 reservation." Your reservation sheet should confirm this.

The Maître d' or Dining Room Manager may have pre-assigned specific tables for the reservations. If this is the case, escort Mr. Smith and his party to the table that's been indicated.

Sometimes you won't be able to locate a reservation on the reservation sheet. Often several people take reservations over the course of the day. Someone may have written the reservation in the wrong time block or wrong day of the week. I almost hate to say this, but sometimes a guest really *hasn't* made a reservation and says he has in order to get a table in a popular restaurant on a busy night. Don't panic. Do the best you can to accommodate the guest and apologize for any inconvenience.

Guests without reservations must be treated courteously and not like second-class citizens. The first thing to do is ask how many guests are in the party so that you know how large a table you'll need to accommodate them. If the restaurant is not busy, great. Reply with, "We're delighted to have you here. Please give me a moment to find you a table."

If the restaurant *is* busy, ask for a few moments to double-check the reservation sheet in order to find a table. If you believe a table will be available in a reasonable amount of time, start a waiting list or add the name to your existing waiting list.

Maintaining a waiting list - Sometimes a guest will come into the restaurant without a reservation. He'll look around the dining room and see many vacant tables. You may *still* have to tell him that you have nothing available at that moment. The guest may then ask why he can't have one of the empty tables. Politely inform him that those tables have been reserved. Ask if he'd like his name to be placed on the waiting list.

Sometimes tables are not seated because the restaurant is short-staffed or the crew is overwhelmed and can't handle the business they already have. If you seat a guest at this point, they'll inevitably receive poor service. It's usually better to ask them to wait a few minutes rather than seat them and hope for the best. I don't suggest sharing this internal concern with the guest. Just ask them to wait.

A waiting list will look very similar to a reservation sheet. It should have the guests' time of arrival, the number in the party, some description of the guest so that you can later locate him when his table is ready. Be careful with this last item. Make sure that your little reminder of the appearance of the guest is positive. You never know who might get a glance at your comments. For example, "Balding guy with ugly green jacket," is probably not a very good idea. "Man in dark green jacket," is much better. You get the idea!

Often guests are invited to have a seat in the lounge while waiting for their table. Sometimes this is a restaurant management ploy to get guests to spend money on cocktails before they get to the table. Most times it's a genuine offer to make them comfortable during their wait.

Always give the guest a reasonable estimate of the time a table may be ready for him – but try to estimate high. If you think that a table will be available in fifteen or twenty minutes, tell the guest it'll be ready within half an hour. If you tell the guest fifteen minutes, he'll start asking for his table in ten minutes because it already seems like an hour to him. If, on the other hand, you've given him a half hour estimate and his table is ready in fifteen minutes, he'll be delighted.

Creating balanced stations - The hostess acts as a traffic director, evenly distributing guests throughout the dining room so that one

"Walk this way . . ."

Whenever I speak of what, in the restaurant business is often called "The Walk" (leading guests to the table), I'm reminded of this story:

A curvaceous hostess in high heels, hips swaying as she led a group of guests to the table, said, "Walk this way."

Observing the exaggerated swivel in her step, one guest couldn't help replying, "No way . . . I can't!"

server isn't overwhelmed, while another is standing around looking for something to do.

One way to do this is to draw up a map of the stations and move a small object (a penny is often used) from station to station as you seat the incoming parties. The station on which the object rests is the one where a party has just been seated.

Another way is to create a chart with all of the servers' names and put a mark below the server's name for each guest that's seated in his station. This, too, lets you rotate through all of the stations as you're seating parties.

These methods not only help you keep the dining room organized and the guests evenly distributed, but it's an indication to the servers that they're receiving their fair share of the business during their shifts.

Leading the guest to his table - Make eye contact with the guest and say, "Please follow me," or "This way, please." Walk in front of the guest, to show him to the table. Move at a steady pace – not too fast. Point out any potential obstacles, "Be careful, there's one small step here." Look back occasionally to make sure the guest is still following you. It's *really* embarrassing to be leading a guest to a table and lose him – you've arrived at your destination, but the guest hasn't. He may have stopped to speak with someone he happens to know.

Seating - If both table and booth seating are available, you might ask for the guest's preference. Try to seat elderly or physically-challenged people at tables where they don't have too far to walk. Seat the booths/banquettes first. People generally prefer booths over tables. When seating at a freestanding table, pull out the chair at the best seat for the first lady to arrive at the table. Good seats are those with the best view – a window, indoor fountain, facing the entertainment, etc. Other preferred seats are those that are out of the traffic flow and those with a back against a wall. Seat ladies to the right of men. Sometimes guests will choose other seating arrangements. Do whatever makes them comfortable.

In some restaurants, the hostess is asked to place the napkin in the guest's lap. Do this quickly and without waving it around. Others limit this practice to female guests only. If the guest extends his hand to take the napkin from you, let him place it in his lap himself, rather than doing it for him.

Adjust the settings – It's always best to seat guests at a table that's been preset for the number of people in the party. This makes the guest feel that the table has been set and made ready specifically for them. If you don't have a table that's already set for the number in a party, ask them to wait so you can adjust the settings. This isn't always feasible. Sometimes it's best to just go ahead and seat the guests, making the adjustment at that time. If you're seating a party of four, for example, it's better to seat them at a table that has been preset for five rather than one that's been preset for three. It's always easier and quicker to remove a setting than it is to add one.

If you've seated a smaller party at a table that's been preset for a larger party, remove the extra setting(s). I think it's a nice touch, after removing the setting, to move all of the center pieces (salt and pepper, sugar, candle) into the space vacated by the removed setting. This helps to rebalance the table. If the tabletop include flowers, this movement will enhance the guests' ability to converse, not having to talk over or through the floral arrangement.

Handing out menus - In many restaurants, the hostess carries the menus with her when seating the guests. Once they're seated, she hands the menu to the guest from the guest's left. Offer women the menus first, then circle back around and give the men their menus, finishing with the host. In very fine restaurants, there are often some menus available without prices. When these are to be presented, this arrangement is made ahead of time by the host. In this case, ladies will receive unpriced menus; sometimes all of the guests will. The host will always receive a menu with prices. The reason for this? A gracious host won't want his guests to concern themselves with prices, or allow pricing to determine their dining choices.

Additional duties – It's important that a hostess be able to answer the guests' questions about the restaurant's facilities and staff: "The restrooms are down the hallway on your left." "The phone is behind the counter." "You'll need to dial '9-9' to get an outside line." "The Chef studied at the Culinary Institute of America and has been cooking here for four years." Other questions may be about the general locality and places of interest.

You may be asked to assist in clearing and resetting, especially if a guest is waiting for a table. You may also be involved in servicing the check. When you have guests waiting to be seated, and you're trying to pare down your waiting list, you'll be glad to pitch in and do these things.

Make sure to say good night to each and every guest as he leaves the restaurant. Thank guests for dining with you. Extend an invitation to return soon. The goodbye is *at least* as important as the greeting. It's the last impression that the guest will take away with him.

Once the host or hostess has seated the guests and started them on their way to a pleasant dining experience, it's then up to the service team to guide them through the courses of the meal. To understand how the meal should flow, it's helpful to know a bit about the types of menus and what they might offer . . .

Chapter 14

"When do I serve the soup?":
courses of the meal and menu construction

In this chapter, we'll look at the different types of menus, how a menu is constructed and the various courses of a meal.

The menu as we know it today – a sheet of paper or cardstock presented to each guest, listing the various choices – is a relatively modern invention. Prior to this, the menu was usually in the form a large poster placed just inside the door of an inn or eating house. It listed the few options available to the diner.

Types of menus

Static - offers the same dishes every day and is used in most restaurants. The menu will change perhaps once or twice a year. The specials of the day are listed on a board, as an attachment to the menu, or given orally. Specials help to offer a variety and a change for the "regulars" – those who frequent the restaurant on a regular basis. By offering daily specials, the kitchen staff has the opportunity to use up its inventory. They're also able to buy what's fresh and in season and purchase at the best prices.

Cyclical - changes every day for a certain period of time. It's generally based on a seven or 14 day cycle. For example, if the restaurant is on a 14 day cycle and a diner is having the spaghetti and meatballs on a Monday, he can expect to see it on the menu again on Monday, two weeks later. Guests who have a favorite menu item know which day to expect it and can plan their visits to the restaurant accordingly. Schools, hospitals and industrial feeders are most likely to use a cyclical menu.

À La Carte - Items are listed separately and priced separately. The customer selects items to form his own meal. This is the most common way that restaurant menus are structured. It may be a static menu though, in an upscale restaurant, the menu could change daily and might be handwritten by the chef.

Prix Fixe *(PREE fix)* - is a multi-course meal, offered at a set price. I've seen as many as ten courses on a Prix Fixe menu and as few as three. A guest will usually have an option or two for each menu course. It doesn't matter which choices he makes, the price of the meal remains the same. Some restaurants will offer two different Prix Fixe menus; maybe one with five courses and one with seven. The guest can choose his meal according to the size of his appetite and how much he wants to spend.

Often, restaurants will also match a wine with each course and offer this as an add-on to the Prix Fixe meal. Since few diners want to consume five, seven or more full glasses of wine with their dinner, the pours will typically be two or three ounces at the most, giving the guest just a few sips to enjoy with each course.

Table d'Hôte *(TAHB luh dote)* - is a multi-course meal offered at a set price. It differs from a Prix Fixe menu in that the price of the entrée determines the price of the meal. The price of the meal is listed next to the entrée. For example, a five course chicken dinner might be $50, whereas a five course lobster meal might be $80, or $110 if you chose to add-on the wine option.

Menu Construction

A menu is a sales tool. It is *not* set up arbitrarily. It's organized in such a way as to sell food.

Appetizers, soups/salads and entrées are usually listed separately. Some menus have individual entrée sections for seafood, poultry and meats. Desserts are often listed on their own menu and presented at the appropriate time.

The general rule is to showcase the entrées, which are usually the most expensive items on the menu. On a single page menu, entrées would start about a third of the way down the page (following the appetizers, soups and salads). On a two page menu (one with left- and right-hand pages), the entrées would most likely begin at the top of the second page. Traditionally, lighter food is listed before heartier fare. Sometimes cold and hot foods are listed separately.

Legendary French chef Fernand Point (under whom world-renowned Chef Paul Bocuse trained) observed that "every menu has three purposes: to please the eye, to trigger the appetite and to

**"Order??? . . .
I can't lift the *menu*!"**

According to Emile Goudeau, restaurant menus in the 19th century were huge and may have contained as many as "a hundred soups . . . three hundred entrées, two hundred roasts, four hundred side-dishes and two to three hundred wines."[8]

Talk about having trouble deciding what to order!

let people know how much of their money they are about to spend." The most important function "is that of pleasing the eye and the other senses," said Point, "for if the menu is not appealing, the people will lose their appetites and their desire to part with their money."[9]

Courses of the meal

You may have heard of seven or maybe even ten course meals. How many courses of a meal can you name?

Traditionally, a formal French banquet would consist of 13 courses.[10] In the Abruzzi region of Italy, there's a traditional meal called a "panarda" that consists of 30 courses!

Listed here are the most common courses served in an upscale restaurant, along with some of the dishes that would be served in each category. You'll note that many of the items are French preparations, since this is the classic cuisine often served in a fine dining establishment. You may never encounter these particular dishes, but it's helpful to know what they are and when they're served during the meal.

Appetizer - A food item that's served before a meal, to stimulate the appetite. It can be either hot or cold. Generally, a small portion is served.

Caviar - the salted roe (eggs) of the sturgeon. The small spheres have a crisp texture that "pops" in the mouth. It has a pleasant, salty taste. Generally accompanied by toast points, cooked chopped egg yolks and egg whites, chopped onions, and parsley.

Pâté - a finely ground, seasoned meat filling sometimes wrapped in pastry, served either hot or cold.

Foie Gras - the enlarged liver of a goose or duck. It has two smooth, rounded lobes and an extremely high fat content. Generally seared and served warm.

Gravlox - A Swedish dish of salmon that has been cured in a sugar, salt and dill mixture, sliced thin.

Other traditional appetizers:
Coquille St. Jacques
Quiche Lorraine
Oysters on the Half Shell
Shrimp Cocktail
Oysters Rockefeller

Soup - a liquid food derived from meat, poultry, fish and vegetables. Most soups are served hot. There are, however, several soups that are served cold.

Hot Soups:

>*Bouillon* - A clarified soup generally made from beef or chicken stock.
>
>*Consommé* - A clarified (usually) chicken stock that has been reduced and concentrated.
>- Celestine - with crêpe strips
>- Xeres - with sherry
>
>*Chowder* - a chunky, hearty soup
>- Manhattan Clam Chowder
>- New England Clam Chowder
>- Corn Chowder
>
>*Bisque* - a soup made from the shells of shellfish
>- Lobster Bisque
>- Shrimp Bisque
>- New Brunswick Scallop Bisque

Cold Soups:

Vegetable-based
- Gazpacho - Spanish tomato & vegetable
- Vichyssoise - French potato & leek
- Borscht - Russian beet

Fruit-based – usually made with heavy cream. Much like a smoothie. Berries, melon, bananas, pears, apples and many other fruits can be used.

Fish Course - a relatively small portion of fish, delicately presented. If a fish course is part of the menu, then the main course should not be fish.

Salad - assorted greens and dressing. May be served before or after the main course. Salad served before the main course is more common in America, but is a relatively recent tradition. In Europe, it's usually served after the main course to refresh the appetite before the cheese and sweet courses that follow.

Salads fall into two basic categories: *tossed* and *composed.*

> *Tossed salads* are just that, ingredients added to a bowl and tossed to distribute the dressing.
> • Caesar
> • Spinach

> *Composed salads* are those in which the ingredients have been artistically arranged on the plate, usually on a base of lettuce.
> • Asparagus
> • Seville (Orange, Avocado & Onion)

Sorbet – a small portion of flavored ice, served after the salad and before the entrée. It's meant to "cleanse the palate" (the roof of your mouth that you touch with your tongue). Most salad dressings are made with oil and an acid (vinegar, lemon juice, etc.). Salad oil has a tendency to stick to your palate. Sorbet is meant to refresh the palate and prepare it for the entrée. It's served after the fish course if the salad is presented after the entrée.

Sorbets are made from fruits, liqueurs and some wines. Most commonly, they're citrus (orange, lemon, grapefruit). These fruits have a natural acidity which helps to rinse away the oil of the salad dressing.

Entrée - the main course of the meal. Meat, poultry and fish are the most common choices, often served with a sauce. The entrée plate usually includes a vegetable and sometimes a starch, such as rice, potato or pasta.
- New York Steak au Poivre
- Duck a l'Orange
- Sole à la Meunière

Dessert - The sweet course. This could include: pastries, tarts, cakes, tortes, soufflés, mousses.
- Eclair
- Black Forest Cake
- Grand Marnier Soufflé

Cheese and Fruit - composed of several cheeses, usually some hard and some soft.

Hard cheeses
- Parmesan
- Belle Paese
- Gouda
- Cheddar

Soft cheeses
- Brie
- Camembert

Usually the cheeses are accompanied by fruits such as apples, pears and grapes, as well as some kind of bread or crackers.

Beverages – These beverages are typically served at the end of the meal: coffee, decaffeinated coffee, espresso, cappuccino, latte and various teas.

Gourmandises (also called Mignardises or Friandises) - presented with the guest check. Said to "sweeten the check." These might include: chocolates, truffles, palmiers, chocolate-covered strawberries, mints and petits fours.

Knowing your menu, and what your restaurant offers for each course of the meal, can make you a valuable resource to your guests, particularly those with special needs . . .

Chapter 15

Don't feed the guide dog . . .
and other helpful hints for
serving special needs guests

You may find that for, one reason or another, certain guests need a little extra attention. I'm sure you can think of several groups that fall into this category: guests with a physical disability; those with dietary concerns and restrictions; a guest who takes ill; younger children or geriatrics (older people). I like to add to that list the solo diner – the person who eats by himself.

Children - Try to be patient and pleasant with children in your station. A parent can tell when you're annoyed by their children's behavior and it may be reflected in your tip.

When the family is seated, greet the child but don't fuss over him. You don't want to be his buddy. Playing "peek-a-boo!" while you're trying to work can grow old quickly.

Suggest a booster chair for small children. Ask if you may assist the child. Make sure to push the chair as close as possible to the table. This will prevent food from dropping on the floor. If the restaurant doesn't have a booster chair, (with the permission of the parent) use a thick telephone book. Sometimes it's possible to stack two chairs to raise the child to table level, but be sure that this creates a stable seat. If a highchair is used, make sure it's clean before placing it at the table. It's best to allow the parent to secure the child in the highchair.

An infant in a car seat can be a concern. I don't like to see babies placed on the floor – it's too unsanitary and dangerous. Parents sometimes pull two chairs together and rest the car seat between them. This, too, can be risky. Check to see if there's a banquette available. If so, move the party there. The parents can then place the car seat next to them and feel secure. Banquettes and booths are really the best options for parents with small children.

If possible, seat a child by a window or wall. In this position, he can concentrate on his food without being distracted by activity in the room.

Move potential "problem" items. As soon as the child is seated, inconspicuously move the salt, pepper, sugar – and especially the candle, if one is on the table – out of his reach.

Find a way to keep the child occupied. Many restaurants provide "busy" materials for children. These are sometimes in the form of a special children's menu or even the placemat itself. In any case, bring the child a crayon and paper for coloring or something else to keep him occupied. Bring crackers or some kind of bread right away.

Serve young children's beverages in small, juice-sized glasses. If available, plastic drinkware is an even better idea. Don't overfill.

Always bring extra napkins.

Look to the adult for the child's order. When taking the child's order, always take it from the parent unless the adult indicates that you're to take the order from the child.

Ask the parent if it's okay to bring the child's food as soon as it's ready. This can help keep the child calm and busy. Sometimes, though, the parent will ask that the child be served at the same time as the rest of the guests.

You'd be surprised what some children will order ... and eat.

I was working in a very upscale restaurant and the guest had indicated that the child would do his own ordering. When he began with "I'll have the escargots," I did a double-take. Glancing over to mom, she gave me a look of pride that said, "He knows what he likes." When the snails arrived, he knew exactly how to deal with them and proceeded to devour them in short order. Maybe that saying about little boys being made of "snails and puppy dog tails" isn't so far off!

Remember, for the safety of the children and other guests, we have to do our best to keep the children contained and not running around in the restaurant.

Guests with special diets - When a guest mentions that he has special dietary concerns, take that seriously. These concerns can range from basic dislikes and religious taboos to life-threatening allergic reactions. Listen to the guest carefully and make sure you understand his specific concerns.

serving special needs guests 133

Don't presume to know everything that goes into the preparation of the food. Always double-check with the chef: "I don't think that soup has any pork in it, but let me check with the chef to make sure."

Guests with medical conditions may ask for your assistance when ordering. Diabetics are concerned about the sugar content of the food; people on low cholesterol diets, the amount of saturated fats. Guests with high blood pressure will be looking for items that are low in sodium.

Guests with dietary restrictions due to religious beliefs might also need assistance. Hindus don't eat beef; Moslems and some Jews don't consume pork.

Vegetarianism is becoming very popular again. When a guest states he's is a vegetarian, ask what he does and doesn't eat. This will help you make better suggestions.

Vegans (VEE-gans) are pure or strict vegetarians. They eat only fruits, vegetables and grains. They eat no animal foods such as meat, poultry, fish, eggs or dairy products.

Lacto vegetarians consume dairy products in addition to plant foods. They don't eat eggs, meat, poultry or fish.

Ovo-lacto vegetarians eat eggs and dairy products in addition to plant foods. They don't eat meat, poultry or fish.

Still others who consider themselves vegetarians permit a little seafood in their diet.

Be creative in making your suggestions once you know the guest's restrictions. Often, dishes can easily be altered by eliminating something in the preparation. Always check with the chef and find out what's possible.

I've had an extended family of Sikhs (an Indian religious sect) as regulars because I took the time to learn their diet and could make proper suggestions and accommodations. By the way, they were *very* good tippers!

Guests with allergies - When a guest says he has an allergy to a specific food, that's much different from a like or dislike. Food allergies can cause anything from a simple case of hives to a trip to the hospital – and potential for even worse. The most common food allergies include: milk, chocolate, peanuts, shellfish and gluten (an ingredient in most flours).

Always double-check every item that the guest with allergies has ordered to be sure that his food is safe for his consumption. Never make assumptions. Always ask the chef. For example, a guest has ordered chicken salad. You know that you've never seen peanuts on the salad, but what you may *not* know is that peanut oil may have been used in the dressing.

Allergies have been known to be so severe that just the smell of some foods can cause an allergic reaction. I know of one case where the aromas of a sizzling shrimp platter, just passing by the table, sent a guest to the hospital!

Geriatric guests – Sometimes older people can be difficult to serve. Try to have some patience. Treat them as you'd want a server to treat *your* grandparents. Most of the time, they may not even realize that they're being difficult.

When assisting an older person in ordering, make sure they're aware that particular items are especially spicy or highly seasoned: "You know that dish is quite spicy, right?"

Older people are sometimes overwhelmed when a huge plate of food is placed in front of them. If you know that an ordered item is especially large, advise him of that, or perhaps suggest that a couple share one entrée.

Physically challenged guests - Over the course of a career, you may serve guests with physical disabilities. We'll touch on several specific challenges, with general suggestions . . .

> *Visually impaired guest* - Many blind people carry collapsible white canes. This may help you to identify a guest who might need special assistance.

If a visually impaired guest comes to the table with items such as a purse, briefcase or coat, try to keep all of these belongings together for easy retrieval.

Lead the blind person. Offer your arm for the guest to grasp. Let them make the initial contact with you. Walk slowly, side-by-side. Seat visually impaired guests in a well-lighted area. If the guest is accompanied by a service animal, don't pet or attempt to be friendly with it. And don't feed the animal – he's on duty! It *is*, however, appropriate to ask the guest if you can provide a small bowl of drinking water. Also be sure to seat the guest in an area where there's adequate room for the service animal to be comfortable.

Quietly remove all objects that could be toppled easily by the guest (vase, candle, extra glasses or silverware).

Some restaurants have menus written in Braille or have large-print menus available. Ask the guest, "Do you take a menu?" I know this may sound peculiar, but many legally blind people have limited sight and are able to read a menu. Have a pen light available for the guest's use. If he can't read the menu, mention several of the items, along with the prices. Don't offer suggestions unless asked to do so because there may be some items that the guest can't handle easily and may wish to avoid in a restaurant setting.

Always try to be alert to the needs of the blind guest. Don't overfill beverage glasses. Bring only the silverware that's needed for the dish that you're presenting. Let him know, in a low voice, that you're placing his food in front of him. Try to make all of your movements around the table slow and graceful; avoid quick, jerky movements.

If you feel that assistance may be needed with removing a bone or cutting meat into bite-sized pieces, suggest that you'll have it done in the kitchen. You don't want to be standing alongside the guest cutting his food for him. The guest doesn't want that either. Remain close to the table to assist if you're needed.

Many blind guests place their hands on the dinner table. Gently touch the tips of the guest's fingers with the beverage glass or coffee cup, saying, "Here's your water glass, sir." A blind guest will find this helpful.

When delivering food, announce yourself. "Excuse me, here's your dinner." Ask the guest if he'd like you to describe the placement of the food on his plate. If so, describe the food using the "face of the clock" method: "The steak is at 6:00, the potatoes are at 10:00 and the vegetables are at 2:00."

If the guest pays with a credit card, assist in placing his hand with the pen at the signature line on the voucher. If he pays with cash, be aware that he knows one bill or coin from another. He has generally been assisted in advance in folding different denominations of bills in various configurations. Count back his change as you place it in his hand.

When he's ready to leave, gather up the guest's belongings and ask if he'd like assistance in putting on his coat.

Hearing impaired guest - If you're aware of a guest's hearing impairment, seat him in a quiet, well-lighted area of the restaurant. If you observe that the guest is lip-reading, face him, speak slowly and enunciate clearly. If a guest doesn't speak, offer a pad and pen to make communication and ordering easier.

Be sensitive to clues when you suspect that a guest may be hard of hearing. If you observe that a guest doesn't respond to a question, or you hear, "What did you say?" often, the guest might have difficulty hearing. To get this guest's attention, gently tap him on the shoulder to let him know you're there to take his order.

Guest in a wheelchair - Choose a table that's close to the entrance of the restaurant so it's more convenient for, and calls less attention to, the guest.

Be aware that it's not easy to maneuver guests in wheelchairs up or down stairs. I've been in the position, in a multi-tiered restaurant, where it was necessary to lift (with the assistance of another staff member) a guest in a wheelchair up or down several steps. Not a very good idea for either the guest or staff – and think of the liability issues!

Often, a guest in a wheelchair will call ahead to alert the staff. If you know that he's going to remain in the wheelchair at the table, remove a chair and make space available, in advance of the guest's arrival. Also remove any other unnecessary chairs. Adjust the other settings so that the guest in the wheelchair will have a little more room at his setting. Wheelchairs are generally quite a bit wider than a typical dining room chair.

Make sure that the position you've chosen for the guest in a wheelchair is out of the flow of traffic. The best placement for this guest is with his back to a wall. If the guest wishes to sit at a regular chair, ask if you may be of assistance to him. Don't pull the guest up. Allow him to do that himself. Follow the guest's directions on how to assist.

Place the wheelchair out of the way. Make sure that several service people know where you have relocated it. A manager should also be informed. This is also true when a guest is using crutches. They should be placed so that no one trips over them.

Make sure that the crutches or wheelchair are available immediately to the guest when he's ready to leave.

Guests who take ill – Unfortunately, guests occasionally become ill while in a restaurant – sometimes *seriously* ill. Here are some general suggestions in case of a heart attack, epileptic seizure or fainting.

Remain calm and take charge. Don't attempt to move the ailing guest. If he's fallen to the floor, place a cushion (or a rolled up tablecloth, jacket, or whatever you can find that's clean and soft) under his head. Remove any chairs or objects that are close by.

Call for a supervisor. Follow whatever emergency procedures your restaurant has put in place. Don't attempt to give first aid, other than the Heimlich maneuver, in case of choking (and only if you've been trained). Reassure the guest that help is on the way.

Solo diner - The two largest groups of solo diners are the elderly and the business traveler.

More than 24 million Americans live by themselves. Of the 31.8 million Americans who are 65 and older, about 16% of the men live alone and about 42% of the women.

Americans make more than 35 million business trips a year. The average trip lasts four days. More than 70% of business travelers make their trips alone.[11]

It's sometimes easy to overlook the solo diner when you think strictly in terms of tips, but remember – the business traveler may eat by himself this time, but the next time he may bring in a party of 20 and ask for your station if you've treated him well.

Some restaurants have been experimenting with "networking" or "community" tables where solo diners can choose to be with other guests if they desire company. When you're serving a community table, try to introduce people to one another.

When greeting a solo diner at the door, never say, "Party of one?" Consider how that might make the guest feel.

Place single diners at a table set for two (a "deuce" in restaurant lingo) in a nice area of the restaurant. Occasionally set only one place setting.

Place a single diner in a very visible spot. Have some reading material available. Seat the solo diner where there's something "visual" going on – facing an exhibition kitchen or at an oyster bar, for example.

An experienced, professional server should be assigned to the table. This server should recommend split portions or suggest smaller servings. Solo diners may want to sample several appetizers rather that have a traditional meal. Elderly diners will particularly appreciate the smaller portion options.

A restaurant that wishes to cater to the solo diner will have a wine list with a variety of wines by the glass or by the half bottle. Some restaurants offer 2-to-3 ounce "flights" of wine; usually three different wines to accompany a course. Appetizer and dessert samplers, with several selections offered in smaller sizes on a single plate, are a nice option for the solo diner.

If you notice that people at a neighboring table are starting to bother or make unwanted advances toward someone dining alone, discreetly offer to move the solo diner to another table immediately.

Occasionally, with the prior approval of the manager, send a complimentary dessert or glass of wine (known as a "comp" in the business) to the "regular" solo diner. Remember, a server can't usually authorize a comp – it has to be done by the manager. You can suggest it, however: "That single gentleman has been here twice this week. May I comp him a dessert?"

And, since we're on the subject of regular guests, what *can* you do to help your restaurant build up a steady clientele? Let's look at some of the factors that make guests want to return . . .

Chapter 16

"So nice to see you again . . . ":
why guests become "regulars"

There are so many options available to the diner today. How does a restaurant stand out from its many competitors? What makes a customer want to return to a restaurant time after time and become a regular?

Regulars are the mainstay of a restaurant. Seasonal tourists and their business will come and go but local, repeat customers are a restaurant's "bread and butter". Guests return because they've enjoyed the experience.

Some of the reasons guests become regulars . . .

Food – Obviously, the guest returns to a restaurant because he enjoyed the food that he was served there. You, as the server, have the opportunity to do a final quality assurance check before serving the food. Look at each plate before serving it. If the food has shifted during delivery, discreetly reposition it if possible. When you can't, have the food replated in the kitchen. Make sure there are no drips or fingerprints on the plate rim. Double-check to make sure the guest is receiving the correct food. Is the order complete? Does it have all of the side dishes? Is everything on the plate that's supposed to be there?

Hey! Where's the meat?

I once had a server present six Reuben Sandwiches (a grilled sandwich featuring rye bread, corned beef, Swiss cheese, sauerkraut and thousand island dressing) to a table of gentlemen. The cook had forgotten to put the corned beef on the sandwiches! A more experienced server might have noticed the omission before serving it.

The first thing a guest will check when his food is delivered is whether what's on his plate is what he ordered. Next, he'll probably notice the presentation of the food. As many chefs will tell you, a guest eats with his eyes before he eats with his mouth. Is the meal attractive and neatly plated? Or, does it appear to have been plopped onto the plate? The diner will also notice the aromas of the food. The sense of smell is essential to the tasting of food.

A chef might be compared to an artist, with the plate as his canvas. When he decides how he wants a plate to look, he takes into account a number of factors. Is the presentation colorful? Are the various colors placed next to others that will complement them? He'll also consider the shapes of the items on the plate, trying to vary them as much as possible. If, for example, he's serving a chopped steak, generally oval in form, he most likely won't choose a potato that's similarly shaped. Food textures are another factor when deciding on plating. If he's using a puréed vegetable, the chef won't likely pair it with mashed potatoes – he'll use something with a little more "crunch". It makes for a more interesting taste experience.

The look and aroma of the food are two more examples of "first impressions" and how your guests' perceptions can be altered either positively or negatively by what's placed in front of them.

Good perceived value - is essential for a quality restaurant experience. Was the meal that you received worth what you paid for it? This could be applied to any level of dining.

In a fast food restaurant, you'll decide whether the five dollars that you spent for a "meal deal" is worth five dollars. Was it fresh? Was it enough food in relationship to what you paid?

In a fine dining establishment, you might spend $50 per person for dinner. Here, other factors have to be taken into consideration. Portion size is not nearly as important to most people in this case as is the quality of the product and the skill with which it was prepared. Service in an upscale restaurant plays a large role in the perceived value of a dining experience.

Service - As mentioned earlier, 60% of all complaints in a restaurant are based on the guest's perception of inadequate or poor service. On the other hand, many surveys have shown that good service is most often mentioned as a reason for guests' return visits. People like to feel welcome and comfortable at a restaurant where they choose to spend their money on a regular basis.

Guests notice and appreciate a ready smile from the service team.

When both your wallet and your stomach are empty, something's wrong . . .

I remember, as a child, eating at what I thought was a very fancy restaurant while my family was vacationing in Florida. It was one of those Polynesian-themed places so popular in the '60s. My dad ordered a ton of dishes so we could try a lot of different things. I remember thinking how expensive it all was. When we got back in the car, we decided, by unanimous vote, to stop at a nearby hamburger joint. We were all still starved! A perfect example of poor perceived value.

They want to be acknowledged quickly after being seated. When you're able to greet a regular by name, that goes a long way – a person's favorite words are his own name. If your restaurant allows, cheat a little bit. Check the reservation sheet. See who's scheduled to be in your station that day. Maybe it will bring back some memory of the last time the guest was in. My friend, Mr. Louie, would remember a guest's food and drink preferences from the last time that he had dined in his station, even when it had been months – or sometimes years – before. This made him an extremely popular restaurant server and host and, needless to say, Mr. Louie always made great tips!

Product knowledge is the keystone of good service. A guest appreciates a server who's knowledgeable about the menu. A server who makes recommendations based on what he believes the guest will enjoy, is a server who'll have repeat customers ("call parties").

A pleasant server is a popular server. A server's job can be trying. The guest must never suspect that you're feeling stress. Be confident. Take charge of the table. Make the guest feel that he's in good hands for the evening. Read the table – be aware of the timing and pacing of the meal. Juggle all of the elements of your job; prioritize and keep your spirits high. If necessary, as I've mentioned before, *be Pagliacci.*

Ambiance/Atmosphere/Environment - whatever you choose to call it. It's the intangible "feel" of the restaurant. Many elements go into creating the ambiance of a restaurant . . .

Sanitation is a primary concern. The restaurant must always look spotless. Make sure that *your* station is clean. When turning a table, police the area. Remove all items left on or around the table by the previous party. Check out your side station. Reorganize for the next wave of business, if necessary. Complaints from guests about the state of the restrooms should be relayed to a supervisor immediately.

The lighting of a restaurant helps to set the atmosphere. Sometimes specialists in restaurant lighting are hired during the design process to make sure that all areas are illuminated properly. Does management want the restaurant to have a romantic atmosphere? Are they after a bright, open bistro feel? Your part in this: If you see uneven lighting, or bulbs burned out anywhere in the restaurant, inform a manager. If a guest indicates they have trouble reading the menu because the light is too dim, or asks to have an adjustment made because a track light is glaring in their eyes, be sure to relay this to your manager immediately as well.

Make sure tables are picture-perfect. The manner in which the tables are positioned and set is important to the overall feel of the restaurant. Sometimes tables are pulled together to accommodate a large party. After they've gone, return the tables to their original positions. Make sure they're lined up with the adjacent tables. Check the spacing between tables. Double-check your station and your settings. Every setting should be alike. Remember, we're always striving for that feeling of balance, or symmetry.

The temperature in the restaurant either adds to, or detracts from, the general ambiance. Restaurants are generally quite cold. I read recently that, in the opinion of a syndicated columnist, this was a ploy to speed up the turning of the tables. I disagree. I think that restaurants are kept cold because the thermostats are set by the staff, who are usually overdressed in tuxedos or the like and are looking out for *their* comfort. They're working and running around – the guest isn't. If a guest comments on the temperature of the room, make the manager or hostess aware.

Plants and music also add to the feel of the restaurant. Guests' comments about the choice or volume of the music or the general well-being of the plants should be passed on to management.

Location - Real estate brokers are fond of saying that the three most important factors in determining the success of a new restaurant are: location, location, location. It's obvious that you, as a server, can't do anything about the location of the restaurant. You *can* help to put the restaurant "on the map", as it were, by being a part of the team that provides such outstanding food and service that the location becomes unimportant. Guests will find the restaurant if you continue to deliver a great product.

As a server, you're in an enviable situation. Most diners come into a restaurant prepared to enjoy themselves. Unfortunately, this isn't always the case. Some guests present challenges. How do you handle them?

Chapter 17

Handling guest problems and problem guests

Unhappy guests

When a customer goes into a car dealership, he prepares himself for an ordeal – an uncomfortable, stressful experience. He has his guard up. Guests don't usually come into a restaurant with that sort of mindset. They generally start their restaurant experience in a positive, or at least neutral, state of mind.

But every restaurant is going to have a few dissatisfied customers. Our job, as servers, is to minimize that number. Guests who experience unresolved problems may not return. A dissatisfied customer tells an average of 11 other people about his bad experience. When we can't provide a solution to an unhappy guest, we not only lose his business, we may also lose the business we would have received from his friends and family. No restaurant wants this kind of "advertising".

A guest who has voiced a problem, and has it resolved to his satisfaction, will often become a regular. As a server, accept the challenge of turning an unhappy customer into a future call party.

Awhile back, I managed a restaurant with a very young, inexperienced staff. The servers would come to me after a particular guest left the restaurant to say how rude and condescending he was to them. After two or three of these conversations with various servers, I felt it was necessary to speak with this gentleman.

On a subsequent visit, I asked if I might speak with him away from the table before he left. I shared the feelings of my young servers, and asked if he could try to be a little more considerate. I impressed upon him that they were truly trying to do their best. The guest, after a thoughtful pause, thanked me and left. This gentleman became one of the restaurant's best patrons and servers fought over the opportunity to wait on him.

A guest who voices a complaint is actually doing you and the restaurant a favor. He's giving you the opportunity to correct the problem. Many guests don't express their displeasure verbally, they just never return. If you can learn to read the subtle signs, you may be able turn a negative situation into a positive one.

Sometimes you can tell a diner is unhappy with his meal, even though he may not complain. Be sensitive to a guest's unspoken dissatisfaction. These might be some tip-offs:

Avoiding eye contact - If a guest avoids making eye contact with you after being served his food, you might have a customer with a problem.

Looking irritated - It might not be the conversation at the table. It might be the food or the service.

Not starting the meal immediately - Sometimes a guest is in the middle of a conversation when his food is served. He may continue to talk until he feels that he's at a point in the conversation where he can take a break to eat. It might, however, be a comment on the food.

Looking around the room - A moment or two after being served, the guest is looking around the room, trying to locate a server. This may signal a problem.

Asks to see a menu - If the guest asks to see the menu after the food has been served, he probably has a concern. This double-checking indicates that the food sitting in front of him is not what he had in mind when he ordered it.

"Everything is OK" - If this is the guest's response to your check back, it could signal a problem. Depending on the guest's tone, it may be a subtle way to indicate that the food is not completely satisfactory.

Not finishing - This could, of course, simply mean that the guest has had enough to eat. But it could also be indicative of an unhappy diner – one who doesn't like to complain.

If you've ever wondered why some chefs hang out at the dishwashing station, here's the reason: a lot can be learned from a plate when it's brought back into the kitchen. Chefs will try to determine if the portion sizes are too large and that's why the plates are unfinished. If very little has been eaten, they may question the server to see if the guest had a complaint about the food. What's left on plates can also be an indication that the food wasn't prepared properly, wasn't fresh or just isn't a popular menu item or special.

Dealing with the guest problems

Listen to the guest - Follow his description of the complaint, step-by-step. Allow him as much time as he needs. Don't interrupt. Maintain eye contact and use positive body language. Try to get as many specific details as possible. It's a good idea to take notes. Sometimes you may have to involve your manager. If you do, he won't have to go over all of the details a second time with the guest, you will have briefed him. Try to understand the diner's point of view. Don't take the complaint personally.

Apologize for the situation - Restate the guest's remarks in your own words. This way, you know that you've completely understood his concern. Always offer an apology specific to the situation: "I'm sorry that your food was cold." Don't offer excuses: "We were really short-handed today." Never blame another department or employee: "The kitchen burned the first pork chop and had to redo the order." Never suggest that the guest's problem is a common occurrence: "A lot of guests send back their steaks because they've been overcooked." Communicate clearly your desire to correct the situation. Again, show empathy for the guest's situation.

Determine a solution - In your mind, go over all the available options. Remember your restaurant's guidelines. If you think you can handle the situation by yourself, prioritize your options and take action. If the solution isn't within your authority to offer ("I think that item should be removed from the check"), explain to the guest that you'll need to get a manager.

Follow-up - Once action has been taken, follow up with the guest to make sure he's satisfied with the solution. "I'm sorry, again, for the overcooked steak. Are you enjoying the meatloaf?" When suggesting an alternative meal choice, always try to interest the guest in a dish-out item, something that's already fully cooked and ready for plating in the kitchen. This way, the new plate can be delivered quickly and the guest can be eating at the same time as the rest of the party.

Notify the Manager - In all cases, notify your manager of any problems, even if you believe that you've successfully resolved them. If your guidelines don't permit you to solve the problem, involve a manager. After advising the manager of the situation, ask for advice and, if possible, continue to handle the situation yourself. If the manager feels he should take over, make sure he has all the details.

Dealing with problem guests

Occasionally, you'll meet guests who'll truly try your patience. You'll wonder (to yourself, of course!) why these people dine out. You want to receive a tip, but how do you deal with the problems that *they* create?

As a server, always try to handle serious concerns away from the table. It serves no purpose for you and the guest to have an argument in front of the rest of the party. Ask him to please step away from the table so you can best resolve the situation.

In many cases, there are ways to handle the difficult guest and still come out with a tip. Here are a few types of problems and suggestions on how to handle them:

The complainer - Sometimes no matter what you do, you can't seem to please a particular guest. He's just not happy with anything. From the minute he sat down, the two of you seem to have been at odds about everything from the time it took to serve his drink to the fact that his favorite dish isn't on the menu. Don't argue with him. Don't lose your cool. If you're part of a team, let one of the other servers make most of the contact. When all else fails, ask the manager if another server or service team can take over.

The overly-amorous guest - Many men find waitresses attractive and many women find waiters attractive, too. As a server, you may find yourself being asked out or propositioned by a guest (Personally, I can't say that happened often to me!). If you can, handle the situation with a sense of humor. Use a reply like, *"Sure,* if I can bring my *husband (or wife)* a n d *kids."* Tell the guest that you're flattered, then use restaurant policy as an excuse. Most restaurants frown on servers dating guests. Don't get upset, or be rude.

The inebriated guest – You'll know him when you see – or hear – him. He's the guy who's talking much too loud; annoying the

Some guests really "take the cake"
*The host of a party of ten said he'd brought a birthday cake for me to serve after dinner. (Bringing your own cake to an upscale restaurant is really inappropriate, by the way.). I told him I'd take care of it and put the cake in the walk-in. When it was time to serve it, I found that someone had put something on top of the cake – it was a mess! The pastry chef was kind enough to redecorate it but, when I presented the cake, the host went nuts, "That's **not** my cake!," he bellowed. "What are you trying to do?" I explained (away from the table) what had happened and, in the end, the host was pleased with how I'd handled the situation and left an extra large tip.*

other diners around him; stumbling on his way to the restroom and generally behaving as though he's had too much to drink. Because he has. If he wasn't in your station, this scene might be kind of funny. The first step is to bring in the manager, or ask a fellow server for help. If no one is immediately available, handle the situation by yourself but be firm and try not to offend the guest. It may be necessary to ask him to leave because he's become an annoyance to other guests.

The too-comfortable guest - This guest has overstayed his welcome. He parks himself at your best table, alone, orders a cup of coffee and sits. And sits. Sometimes for over an hour with a 95-cent cup of coffee. He may not be annoying, but he's wasting valuable "real estate". That table is worth a lot of money to the restaurant, as well as to you, as a server. Ask him if he'd care for anything else. Clear everything that you possibly can from the table. Present him with a check. You may have to tell him that you're sorry to have to rush him, but if he doesn't require anything else, there are people waiting for a table.

The guest is always right – *right?* - Most restaurants will replace a dish if a customer doesn't like it, even if there's nothing wrong with the food. When a plate is rejected, it's always best to find out why. Was it not what he had expected, from the description? Was it too spicy? Was it cold? After you've determined a cause, ask if he'd like you to replace the food with something else. If it was a steak, for example, and the guest thought it was too tough, I'd suggest that he choose a different entrée since he'd probably find another steak tough as well. Always try to recommend something that's dish-out, or quick to prepare. Inform the manager of the situation.

There are times when, quite frankly, the guest *isn't* right. Say, for instance, you set down the food and check back with the table in a few minutes to see that everyone is happy. All the guests smile or nod. When, later, you're clearing a guest's plate with just bones remaining, and the guest says, "I didn't much care for the chicken," it's really too late to remedy the situation. He's eaten the food and should pay for it.

Or, this example: The guest asks you to substitute one sauce for another. Perhaps he adds or subtracts other ingredients. When he complains later that he didn't like his dinner, he's still responsible for paying for it.

And, how about this one? A guest asks the server about the Thai Flank Steak, "Is it spicy?" The server says, "Yes, it's *quite* spicy." The guest responds, "*Great*, I *love* hot food!" Half way through his entrée, the guest tells the server that the steak is *way* too spicy for him. He asked for it. He got it. He should *pay* for it.

Restaurants thrive through "word of mouth". A satisfied customer tells his friends, family and business associates about his positive dining experience. Try, with whatever means possible under the guidelines of your restaurant, to make every guest a satisfied customer.

In the next few chapters, we'll get into some more advanced subjects and techniques that'll help you become an even *more* polished and professional server and make it even easier to ensure that your guests have a pleasant dining experience.

Chapter 18

Knowing your gin from your "Zin":
alcoholic beverage service

For many guests, a meal just isn't complete without an alcoholic beverage to accompany it. Wines, beers and liquors stimulate the appetite and add a festive note to the dining experience.

Because of their high profit margin, these spirits also add to the check average. To the server, this usually means a bigger tip. One bottle of wine may increase your gratuity more than if your guests ordered an additional food course.

Most servers have a working knowledge of cooking methods and food preparations when they begin their service careers. But they may not know much about alcoholic beverages since many entry-level service jobs are in family restaurants that don't serve alcohol. The transition to an upscale restaurant is easier with a basic knowledge of alcoholic beverage and wine service. Consider the following as a primer. To fully cover this subject would require another book.

Liquor Service

It's important that a good server has a working knowledge of liquors and how they're served. Alcoholic spirits are made from grains and fruits that are fermented and distilled.

Fermentation occurs when the sugars of the raw ingredients are converted into alcohol. This is usually done through the use of a yeast. All alcoholic beverages go through the fermentation process.

Distillation is a process in which the alcohol and the raw materials are separated.

The distilled liquors most commonly consumed today are vodka, gin, whisky, rum, brandy and tequila.

Vodka - is usually distilled from grain mash. It's not aged, as are other liquors. It's colorless, virtually tasteless and has little or no aroma. Because of these characteristics, it's usually combined or blended with other ingredients – with vermouth to make a martini or with orange juice to make a screwdriver.

Gin - is made from barley and rye grains. Like vodka, it's not generally aged. It's colorless, and has a floral taste and aroma. Juniper berries are added for flavoring. Gin is used in much the same way as vodka – add vermouth for a martini; mix with tonic water for a gin and tonic.

Whiskey - means different things to different people in different places. Whiskey produced in the U.S. is called Bourbon *(Makers Mark* is one example*)*; in Canada, it's known as Canadian Whisky, and is spelled without the "e" *(Seagram's V.O.)*; in Scotland, it's Scotch *(Johnny Walker)* and in Ireland, Irish Whiskey *(John Jameson).*

The process for making whiskey is similar to that used to make gin or vodka. It starts as grains, malt is added to turn it into sugar, then yeast converts it to alcohol. Many whiskeys are allowed to age, or mellow, in wooden barrels. Some have caramel coloring added. Whiskeys are usually enjoyed straight or with mixers such as club soda, water, or cola.

Rum - is a by-product of sugar. Sugar cane is crushed, the juice is boiled down, fermented and distilled. It is always aged in wooden casks. The younger rums are used in mixed drinks such as daiquiris (rum, lime juice and sugar) and rum and cola. Rum that has been aged for ten to fifteen years is typically sipped straight. Rums range from the very dark Jamaican style, to the clear rums of Puerto Rico.

Brandy - most often starts as wine (from grapes) and is then distilled. It, too, is aged in wooden casks. It can be enjoyed as a mixed drink, with the addition of water or club soda. It's a fiery liquor and is usually reserved for the end of a meal, when it's sipped straight. Cognac is a very high quality brandy made in the Cognac region of France.

Brandies can also be made from a variety of other fruits. These brandies are usually clear in color and quite potent. They have a very low sugar content. Kirsch is made from cherries; red raspberries are the base for Framboise; Calvados is made from apples; Pear William is made from pears.

How'd that pear get in there???

Pear William has an unusual tale. When a pear tree starts to show fruit, the farmer encases the fruit in a glass bottle and attaches the bottle to the tree. The pear grows inside of the bottle. When the fruit's ripe, the bottle and the pear are removed from the tree. The bottle is then filled with pear brandy.

Tequila - is a Mexican spirit distilled from the fermented sap of the maguey cactus. The core of the plant is cooked, fermented and distilled. Most tequila is not aged and is clear in color. Margaritas are made with tequila, lime juice, sugar and an orange liqueur. The highest quality tequilas are aged in wood. These tequilas take on a golden color and a mellowed flavor. They may be used in mixed drinks but, typically, they're sipped at the end of a meal the same as you would brandy.

Liqueurs and cordials – these terms are interchangeable. Liqueurs are spirits flavored with fruits, aromatic herbs, spices, seeds and flowers. They're generally sweet and reserved for after-dinner sipping. They include Kahlua, Grand Marnier, chartreuse and crème de cassis.

Beer and Ales - Beer is one of the oldest known alcoholic beverages. There are accounts of beer being quaffed in the Bible. It's said that it was Julius Caesar's favorite beverage. Shakespeare's father was the official ale taster of Stratford-on-Avon. And American President James Madison was a brewery owner.

Beer is touted as an appetite stimulant. It's made from malt, hops, yeast and water. Malt, which comes from barley grain, is boiled with water. Hops are then added. The hops are removed and yeast is added to start the fermentation. It's fermented at a low temperature.

Most of the beer that we drink in the United States is lager, which is a light beer and usually includes corn as an ingredient. It's aged in stainless steel tanks.

Ale is similar to beer, but is fermented at a higher temperature and is generally a little more bitter tasting than beer. It's often higher in alcohol content.

Service of alcoholic beverages - A pour (a serving) of liquor is approximately one ounce. It may be served in several ways:

> *Neat* or *straight* - This is the preferred way to enjoy the finest aged spirits. Sipped, not gulped. The aromas are to be savored.

On the rocks (over ice) - This is the most popular way to drink liquors. In an old-fashioned glass, over several ice cubes.

With a mixer - Water, club soda, ginger ale and other mixers are used to dilute the liquor to make it more palatable.

Blended - with fruits, juices, cream or ice cream to make a pleasant, less intoxicating drink.

In most restaurants, there are at least two tiers of liquors. One tier is called "well drinks". This refers to the "speed rail" or "well" that the bartender pours his basic drinks from. The second tier is for "premium pours". The guest either requests, or is asked if he would like to upgrade to, a premium. Scotch and water might become Chivas Regal and water; vodka and tonic, Absolut and tonic. Of course, premium pours are more expensive than well drinks.

It's important that you learn, and use, the standardized abbreviations for drinks that your restaurant has in place. Some basic abbreviations: Rx = rocks, ↑ =neat or straight, Tw or ~ = twist of lemon, W = water, S = soda.

After you've taken a guest's beverage order, leave a beverage napkin or coaster to the right and slightly below the water glass. This is an indication to the manager and other staff that you've

The Main Course on Table Service

been to the table and have taken an order. In some restaurants that use tablecloths, it's policy not to place a beverage napkin or coaster on the cloth. A drink should also not be placed on the show plate.

As in all good service, don't auction off product. Use the same seat designation system that you use for food, only use the back of the guest check for beverages.

Wine

Wine has become more and more popular in the United States in the last twenty years. Wine sales can be an important source of revenue to a restaurant. Some restaurants have wine cellars with thousands of bottles which could translate into millions of dollars in sales. Wine can greatly increase a guest check and, therefore, your tips.

Some upscale restaurants employ sommeliers to order, inventory and assist in selling wines to guests. In most restaurants, the server does his own wine sales and presentation.

Many servers aren't confident in their knowledge when it comes to describing, presenting, opening and pouring a bottle of wine. It really isn't that difficult. Do some reading, and more importantly, do some *tasting*. You'll quickly decide on what you enjoy. That's the first step to assist a guest in choosing a wine.

The globalization of the grape

When I first started in the business in New York, a typical wine list would have 90% French wines. By the mid-'70s, California wines started appearing on lists and California's Simi Cabernet had just defeated French Bordeaux in a head-to-head tasting. Today, wine lists are weighted toward California wines, except at ethnic restaurants which tend to offer wines from their own regions. Wine drinkers are also discovering the wines of Chile, Argentina, Australia and South Africa. You can offer guests terrific wines at great values if you learn more about the wines from these countries.

Wines may be made from many fruits and berries, but the majority are made from grapes so, for our purposes, these are the ones we'll discuss. The juice is pressed from the grapes, fermented and then aged.

Wines may be divided into three categories: table wines, sparkling wines and fortified wines.

Table wines - The majority of wines are considered table wines and are consumed with the meal. These can range from a $15 bottle of White Zinfandel to a $200 Château Lafite-Rothschild (some vintages can run into the thousands of dollars).

Sparkling wines - contain carbon dioxide to make them effervescent, or bubbly. Champagne is a sparkling wine made in the Champagne region of France. Sparkling wines from Spain are known as Cavas.

Fortified wines - Some wines are blended with brandy to make them better suited to storage and transport. Dry fortified wines, such as dry sherry, are served as an aperitif before dinner. Sweet fortified wines, such as port, marsala and madeira and sweet sherries are generally served after dinner.

Characteristics of Wine

Color - Wines are made from red or green grapes. Depending on how they're vinified, the finished product can be white, red or pink (blush). Whites vary from light straw to a rich golden color. Reds range from light, candy apple color to an inky violet. Pinks go from barely tinted to a deep rosé.

Body or viscosity - is the thickness or density of the wine. This can be determined by how it flows around the inside of a glass as it's swirled. A light wine will flow quickly back down to the bottom of the glass. A full-bodied wine will hang onto the side of the glass for a longer period of time. This is sometimes called the "legs" of a wine.

Aroma/bouquet – This is the way a wine smells. It may be fruity, flowery or, sometimes, herbal. Red wines are generally aged and need to open up or "breathe" for several minutes after they've been uncorked to develop their aromas.

Degree of sweetness - Wines can vary from extremely dry to very sweet and everything in between. Drier wines go better with most

David's "Pick 6" ...

When I'm asked to train a service staff about making wine suggestions to guests, I'll take a look at the wine list and "pick six". I'll choose an off-dry white; a light-bodied, dry white; a full-bodied, dry white; a light-bodied, dry red; a full-bodied, dry red; and a popular blush wine. Something from one of these categories can usually be paired with almost everything on the menu. Ask your manager or wine steward for suggestions in each group. You might also want to add a sparkling wine to your list of recommendations.

foods. Sweeter wines pair well with desserts.

Temperatures - The flavor of red wine is at its best when it's served at room temperature. This *doesn't* mean room temperature in Phoenix in June. This really means, "cellar temperature" – between 60° and 70°F. White, pink and sparkling wines are best served chilled, between 45° and 50° F.

The longstanding rule is: dry wines before sweet wines; white wines before red wines; and lighter wines before more full-bodied wines. Keep this in mind when a guest asks for a recommendation.

Following are some guidelines for pairing wine with food. These are traditional matches, but the method of cooking (grilled, poached, etc.) and the sauce served with the dish should be considered when making suggestions. Basically, you're looking for either a complement or a contrast to the food being served. Diners no longer strictly abide by the "white wine with fish, red wine with meat" rule. Instead, encourage your guests to drink what they like, even if it may not be the ideal match for the food they've ordered.

Type of wines	Particular wines	Foods they complement
Appetizer (Aperitif)	Dubonnet Lillet Dry Sherry Sauvignon Blanc	Appetizers, Hors d'oeuvres, Soups
White	Chardonnay White Burgundy Pinot Grigio Riesling	Fish, Shellfish, Poultry, Veal
Red	Burgundy (Pinot Noir) Bordeaux (Cabernet) Zinfandel	Roasts, Steaks, Duck, Stews
Sparkling	Champagnes Cavas	All foods, especially non-chocolate desserts
Dessert	Port Muscat Sweet Sherry Ice Wines	Cheeses, Desserts, Coffees

Wine presentation and service

Offer the wine list to the host or to whomever he asks to select the wine. When the guest has decided, repeat back the name of the wine, as well as the bin number. Wines are often listed by number so the guest doesn't have to pronounce the wine name if he doesn't choose to (it also helps in locating and inventorying wines). You, as the server, on the other hand, should be able to pronounce the names of all of the wines on the list. Have someone on staff work with you if you're not certain of pronunciations.

Present the wine. Approach the guest who's chosen the wine from his right side. Hold the base of the bottle in the palm of your left hand, with a folded, clean napkin beneath the bottle. Hold the neck of the bottle with your right hand. Tilt the bottle so that the guest can easily read the label. This allows him to check if the correct bottle has been delivered. It also allows him to see if the vintage (the year in which the grapes were picked to make the wine) agrees with what's printed on the wine list. Don't shake or make any sudden motions with the wine. There may be sediment in the bottle, especially if it's an old red wine, and you don't want to distribute it throughout the bottle. Announce the name of the wine and the vintage (if there is one). For example, "Here's the 2000 Sonoma Cutrer Les Pierres Chardonnay that you ordered."

Open the wine. I suggest that you uncork the white and blush wines in the wine bucket that's been brought to the table, filled two-thirds with ice and water. Cut the capsule (the foil or plastic that covers the opening of the bottle) with the knife blade of your waiter's corkscrew just below the second ridge in the bottle neck. Turn the blade of the knife, not the bottle. Use the bottom side of the ridge as a guide to get a clean cut. Using the blade, peel back and remove the capsule. Wipe the neck of the bottle with a napkin. Insert the point of the corkscrew in the center of the cork, and twist until the "worm" reaches the end of the cork, or until the corkscrew is fully inserted. Turn the corkscrew, not the bottle.

Red wines should be uncorked on the table. Place your napkin under the base of the bottle. Use the table to rest and support the bottle. Many sommeliers open red wines without having to use the table for support, but it takes a lot of practice to look graceful doing this. Cut the capsule and remove the cork the same way that you would for white wine. Thoroughly wipe the neck of the bottle with your napkin.

Open sparkling wines in the wine bucket. Place the bottle at a 45° angle, facing away from the table. Sparkling wine corks are covered with a wire basket that must be twisted off. Always make sure your hand covers the cork at all times so that it doesn't fly out. Turn the bottle to loosen the cork, don't turn the cork. The cork should come out without a resounding "pop".

Present the cork to the host or the person who's ordered the wine. You can tell a lot about the wine by the condition of the cork. I always pass the cork under my nose before presenting it. If it smells like wine rather than vinegar, the wine is probably fine. I want to know that the wine isn't spoiled before the guest can question it.

Pour a small amount of wine into the host's glass for tasting. While he's holding the glass and swirling the wine, hold the bottle with the label toward the rest of the guests at the table so they know what they'll be drinking. If the taster approves (he'll usually nod or say something like, "That will be fine."), pour the wine for the rest of the guests. Don't wrap the bottle in a napkin. This used to be acceptable procedure, but guests today want to know what they're drinking. Pour the wine with the label facing upward. Time permitting, serve the women first. Don't overfill the glasses. Pour directly into the glass, leaving the glass on the table. Avoid touching the rim of the glass with the bottle. Wipe off the lip of the bottle between pourings. Make sure you remember to fill up the taster's glass!

Continue to pour wine throughout the meal. If someone initially declines wine, ask whether they'll be enjoying a glass at some time during the meal. If not, remove the unused glass. Never finish pouring a bottle into a lady's glass. It's considered bad luck, plus, it will contain whatever sediment or dregs is left at the bottom of the bottle. If possible, finish the wine with the host. This way, he'll be aware that the bottle is empty and can decide whether he wants to order more. The best time to finish pouring a bottle is when the entrée is served. Bring a fresh glass for the host to taste the new bottle. With approval, ask, "May I continue to pour?," then continue. If the host is switching from white to red wine, or from one varietal to another (Merlot to Cabernet Sauvignon, for instance), it's appropriate to change all of the guests' glasses. Remove all bottles from the table as they're emptied.

Though the sale of wines and other alcoholic beverages is an almost effortless way to increase your check average, there are also other effective methods . . .

Chapter 19

Take care of your guests and the money will follow:
the server as salesperson

Is there anyone who *doesn't* want to make more money? If so, I don't think I've met him.

In the restaurant industry, like any other, there's always a way that you can build up your income. On the service side of our business, that usually means increasing tips.

One of the ways to do that is with what many service trainers call *upselling* – creating higher guest check averages by increasing your food and beverage sales.

I prefer, though, to refer to this as *suggestive* selling. To me, *upselling* implies that you're trying to sell a guest something he doesn't really want. I believe that, to be a good salesperson in the restaurant business (and a server really *is* a salesperson), you need to take a genuine interest in giving guests the best possible dining experience. You can do this by making *suggestions* that will enhance their meal and, in turn, increase their tab.

Is the high-ticket item always the best suggestion?

Many restaurant sales training materials will tell you it is. "Always suggest the highest priced food items," they say. "If your guest will like the chicken, think how much happier he'll be with the lobster," they preach.

I strongly disagree. Guests aren't stupid. They *know* when you're just trying to build up the tab. They're going to resent you for it – and they should.

Yes, it's okay to recommend an expensive item to a guest if it's the chef's signature dish or you've had great comments from diners who've eaten it in the past. But don't make that your *only* suggestion. No doubt, there's a lower-end item on the menu that's equally well-prepared or is a guest favorite. Give them the option – they'll appreciate it.

A server whose only interest is in the total of his tips is going to be sorely disappointed when he counts them up at the end of the day.

Use your descriptions to help diners
***taste* the dish before they order it**

In Japan, and in Asian neighborhoods in U.S. cities, restaurants often place replicas of their dishes in their windows (or in some cases, in the entrances) to entice diners into their establishments.

Guests get to see what their meals will look like before they order them.

In most of the rest of the world, though, diners aren't given this advantage. For the most part, it's up to us, as servers, to make menu items sound appealing.

How do you do this? By using descriptive language that paints a picture of the look, taste and aroma of the prepared product. It's really not as difficult as it sounds. It just takes some practice.

Use the sizzle and smell to help you sell . . .

Take the long route through the dining room so more guests can see, hear and smell those sizzling fajitas. Carry the dessert tray a little bit lower and more diners will see how great those sweets look ~ and start deciding what they'll order. Use whatever ways you can think of to awaken your guests' senses to how great your food is ~ and it'll sell itself.

For instance, say the kitchen's offering a special of a pork chop with rice and vegetables. What would you tell your guests about it?

Well first, there are some things you need to know: What is the cut of meat? How is it prepared? Is there a sauce? Is some special ingredient added to the rice or the vegetables? Or is there something unique about where things come from, or how they're handled?

Ask the chef. Get the details. And, suddenly, you're able to tempt your guests' taste buds not just with a pork chop, rice and vegetables but with a *double-cut Iowa loin* pork chop with a *Maytag blue cheese and whole grain mustard sauce,* medley of *Minnesota wild* and *Carolina long-grain* rice with *Georgia* pecan*s* and *locally-grown organic baby* carrots and beets.

Okay, maybe that's going a bit overboard with the description, but you see the point. If you can bring the aromas, flavors and colors of the food to life, your guests are going to want to order the dish.

Though it's a start in the right direction, try not to settle for obvious descriptions like *juicy* pork chop with *fluffy* rice. For one thing, your guests probably *expect* the pork to be juicy and the rice fluffy so it just comes off sounding like phony enthusiasm. In the same respect, don't get so colorful and flowery in your descriptions that you sound like you're reciting a Shakespeare sonnet. Use wording that you're comfortable with – if it doesn't sound natural coming out of your mouth, no one's going to buy what you're trying to sell. And, above all, don't use a "canned" speech to describe your dishes – there's nothing worse for a guest than to hear you give the same rap to him that you just finished at a nearby table.

The same "make it sound great and they'll order it" principle holds true for beverage sales. Don't just ask guests, "Can I get you something to drink?" Why give them the option of ordering an iced tea when they may just as readily order a glass of wine, a beer or a mixed drink if it's offered to them? Ask, "May I start you off with...?," followed by a few specific beverages. Don't just offer a glass of Chardonnay. Offer a buttery, lightly-oaked Kendall Jackson Reserve Chardonnay. Don't just sell them a beer. Make it an imported, amber, full-bodied Foster's lager.

There's no getting around it – good product descriptions take practice to become polished. But really get to know the items you're selling, start slowly by injecting just a few enticing adjectives and you'll be surprised at how soon this can become second nature.

Flexibility leads to greater gratuities

You can't expect every diner at every table to order an appetizer, entrée, side dishes and dessert. For some, it's a matter of appetite – they just can't eat that much – and for others it's a matter of budget – they just can't afford to. That doesn't mean, though, that you can't sell the extra courses.

Suggest that diners split appetizers, desserts or side dishes. When you're able to say, "Let me have the chef prepare a special sampler of our appetizers (or desserts) for you so you can taste some of our specialties," it shows that you're willing to go that extra step for the diners.

If your guests are wavering between ordering several different items, offer to bring them a small sample to try (with the okay of the kitchen staff, of course) before they order. This small gesture and minimal expense goes a long way in selling product.

**Getting your hostess/managers
(and even your bussers!)
to help you sell**

Because you, as a server, have the most direct contact with the diners, it falls on your shoulders to become the primary salesperson. That doesn't mean, though, that other members of your service team can't be called on to help "close the deal."

Your hostess, host or maître d' can inform each table of drink and appetizer specials as the guests are being seated. Your bussers can be trained to offer specialty coffees, desserts and after-dinner drinks. And managers can alert diners to upcoming promotions (wine dinners, special events and holiday celebrations) that may entice diners to return.

Hostesses/hosts/managers should always make servers aware of any special occasions such as birthdays and anniversaries that are being celebrated so the service team is prepared to handle any special requests or requirements. It really helps servers if the hostess or manager also makes them a note with the information since it's very easy to forget a special request in the middle of a very busy shift. Likewise, if they're not already aware, servers should clue the hostess/manager in on any special occasions being celebrated by regular guests so there's an opportunity to "comp" a food item or beverage.

Taking this even one step further, the manager, hostess or even the server may want to compile a list of regular customers' birthdays and anniversaries to send them a greeting from the restaurant on future occasions. This is not only a nice gesture, but also a gentle reminder that they may wish to celebrate at your property. Be sure, though, that the guest *wants* you to know about the occasion – some people can be sensitive, especially about birthdays.

Create your own "call parties"

Some of the most savvy servers I know hand out business cards to their guests. Usually the card is the same one used by the restaurant, but with the server's name imprinted on it. Many times the restaurant will pay for the printing but, even if they don't, as long as management agrees, you may want to consider getting some printed up yourself.

Why hand out cards? Because they help you to market yourself as a professional server and give your guests a personal contact at your restaurant.

When a party has particularly enjoyed a meal, and you've provided them with excellent service, they're likely to return. So why not encourage them to request your station when they do?

Selling not only your food and beverage, but your service

Sure, the ultimate object of selling, as a restaurant server, is to increase the volume of food and beverages consumed. While adding an extra glass of wine or a dessert to a check is the most direct method of doing this, it's not the only way.

Providing your customers with exceptional service is a proven way of generating repeat business. And by building up a regular clientele, you're ensuring that you'll not only be earning good tips today, but next week and next month, too.

Giving exceptional service boils down to one important thing – taking care of the *details*. You need to be observant; anticipate your guests' needs and act on them before they realize it.

This means making sure that they always have the silverware they need for each course; bringing them side plates if they're splitting a dish; not leaving dirty dishes sitting in front of them; bringing them an extra warm-from-the-oven basket of bread without them asking you for it. You get the idea . . . it's the attention to all of the little, easily-missed or ignored details that can set your service apart from the rest.

Remember, a pushy, obvious sales approach might earn you an extra couple of dollars today, but genuine concern that each and every guest has an enjoyable dining experience will translate into repeat business. This will, in the end, bring you the greatest rewards – both in the money you earn and the satisfaction you get from your job.

In the final chapter, I'll give you my own thoughts on what makes a server and his style of service exceptional.

Chapter 20

That extra "something" that makes all the difference:
service above and beyond

Sometimes it takes that little extra "red carpet treatment" to make a diner's experience superlative, not just good. You, as a server, must treat your guests as you'd want to be treated. When it means going above and beyond, and your actions fall within your restaurant's guidelines, do it.

At the Levy Restaurants, based in Chicago, the hosts/hostesses are empowered to do whatever it takes to bring customers back. On occasion, this has meant running after an upset guest in the restaurant's parking lot to try, once more, to resolve an unpleasant situation.

I've known of maître d's who've sent guests' cars out to be washed while they were dining. Once a maître d' at the Waldorf-Astoria in New York personally handpainted a menu for a couple who got engaged there. I recently heard tell of a restaurant manager who, when hearing of a botched "to go" order, took a cab and redelivered the correct order in person. This kindness resulted in a booking of several hundred guests on a subsequent evening.

The principle is this: Give your diners more than they expect and they'll remember you for it.

It may be something as simple as keeping an umbrella by the door for guests to use on a rainy day. Having a pair of non-prescription reading glasses available for the diner who forgot his. Escorting guests to the restrooms instead of just pointing the way. Or sending each diner on his way with a cookie to be enjoyed later.

I'd like to leave you with these thoughts about what I believe constitutes exceptional restaurant service. I don't think that I could express it any better than I did in 1987, when I was named a finalist in the Society for American Cuisine's "Year of the Waiter" essay contest.

Thank you for taking the time to read my book. I hope you feel that you've learned a lot. I wish you luck as you pursue a career in the wonderfully wacky restaurant business.

May your guests be gracious and your gratuities generous!

When I Grow Up
By David Rothschild

Finalist in the Society for American Cuisine's
1987 "Year of the Waiter" Essay Contest

When I was young, I never remember any of the kids dreaming about being waiters when they grew up. I was going to be a lawyer, my friend, Shelly, a banker, and Barry was going to be a doctor. Well, Shelly became a postman, Barry a teacher, and I've been a waiter now for about 20 years.

Many of my fellow waiters today are still dreaming and working toward other careers. I work with aspiring actors, full-time graduate school students and soon-to-be real estate brokers.

Every fine restaurant today, though, has a nucleus of people who have chosen food and wine service as a career and have been at it for a length of time.

Restaurant service is definitely not a career suited for everyone. A waiter has to have a special temperament. He needs to possess a pleasant personality, an even tone and a quiet, dignified manner. He has to have a great deal of patience and the ability to remain poised and unruffled under ever-changing circumstances. I believe that a waiter has to be a giving person, someone with the desire to please.

I like to think of the dining room as "my dining room," and the guests as "my guests." For this night, I am the guide and the host. I try to make the guests feel as if they were in my hands for this evening. I take upon myself a large portion of the responsibility for a diner's positive experience in the restaurant.

A waiter has to be able to gauge the tone of the table; every table is different. I try to determine any time constraints on the diners. If I am really lucky, the patrons will accept my experience and knowledge and allow me to guide them through this dining experience.

A good waiter, in my estimation, is one who is always alert, always aware, yet unobtrusive. In general, I don't believe that a waiter is there to entertain the table. I offer suggestions if asked or, if I determine that the patrons would be receptive, I will then describe, entice and interest a guest in methods of preparation, content and composition of various dishes. I will describe portion sizes, sauces and specials concisely and in a positive manner.

A restaurant's bread and butter is its regular customers; those who return often. I like to think that they return in part because of the service they have received in the past. I try to remember their names and address them by name. It makes them feel even more welcome.

I think if we were to poll a restaurant's regulars as to why they return again and again, service would probably appear as a response at least as often as food or ambiance.

A restaurant prospers because of the good will it creates. The Supreme Court once defined "good will" as follows: "The disposition of the pleased customer to return to a place where he has been treated well."

I think that a waiter has a major role in creating good will and in positively representing ownership and management to the public.

If I please my customers, they return and the restaurant prospers. I am in turn rewarded by having the opportunity to make a decent living while working in an attractive environment.

I enjoy meeting all kinds of different people, talking with them and pleasing them. I like the hours that I work and the flexibility that service allows me.

For the right person, foodservice can be a fun and rewarding career.

Bibliography

1. Montagné, Prosper. *Larousse Gastronomique.* New York: Crown Publishers, Inc., 1961. 214.

2. ibid. 561.

3. 'César Ritz – 1850-1918'. Hotelconsult – César Ritz Hotel Management. URL: http://www.ritz.edu/. 2001

4. URL: http://member.aol.com/acalendar/march/ delmonico.html. 2001

5. Lewis Hotel-Motel Course. *Lesson 33: Lessee, Owner or Operator, Managing Director, Manager.* Washington, DC: Lewis Hotel Training School, Inc., 1967. 1.

6. ibid. *Lesson 1: Outline of the Course.* 89.

7. U.S. Department of Labor Bureau of Labor Statistics. 'Food and Beverage Service Occupations'. URL: http://www.bls.gov/oco/ocos162.htm. 2001.

8. Visser, Margaret. *The Rituals of Dinner: The Origins, Evolution, Eccentricities, and Meaning of Table Manners.* New York: Viking Penguin, a division of Penguin Books USA Inc., 1991. 197. ISBN: 0-8021-1116-5.

9. Rogov, Daniel. 'Rogov's Ramblings'. URL: http://www.stratsplace.com/ Rogov/whats_on_menu.html. 2001.

10. Meyer, Sylvia, Schmid, Edy and Spühler, Christel. Translated by Holtmann, Heinz. *Professional Table Service*. New York: Van Nostrand Reinhold, EnglishTranslation 1991. 71. ISBN: 0-442-23982-3.

11. Stephenson, Susie. 'Seeking Out Singles'. *Restaurants & Institutions*, April 1, 1996. 64.

Other Sources Consulted

The Essentials of Good Table Service. The Cornell Hotel and Restaurant Administration Quarterly. Ithaca, NY: School of Hotel Administration, Cornell University, 1985.
ISBN 0-937056-02-2.

Lehrman, Lewis. *Dining Room Service*. New York: ITT Educational Services, Inc., 1971. ISBN: 0-8455-2403-8.

Harris, Ellen Adeline. *Professional Restaurant Service*. Toronto, Ontario, CA: McGraw-Hill Company of Canada, Ltd, 1966. Library of Congress Catalog Card # 65-29043.

Lefler, Janet, Blanc, Francois and Sack, Louis. *The Waiter and His Public*. Ahrens Publishing Company, 1959. Library of Congress Catalog Card #56-12433.

Dahmer, Sondra J. and Kahl, Kurt W. *The Waiter & Waitress Training Manual*. Boston: Cahners Books International, Inc, 1974. ISBN 0-8436-0575-8.

Gisslen, Wayne. *Professional Cooking*. New York: John Wiley & Sons, 1983. ISBN 0-471-08248-1.

Mario, Thomas. *Playboy's Host & Bar Book*. Chicago: Playboy Press, 1971. Library of Congress Catalog Card # 75-167615.

Restaurants & Institutions. Various Issues

National Restaurant News. Various Issues.

Arizona Republic. Various Issues.

Alexander, Marya Charles. Solo Dining. URL: http://www.SoloDining.com. 2001.

Hughes, Mona. 'Opening Doors'. URL: http://www.home.switchboard.com/ monahughes-writer. 2000.

Index

Brooklyn, 1
Buffet Service, 48
    Advantages, 48
    Disadvantages, 49
business cards, 183
Bussers (buspersons), 17, 34, 49, 85,
    105, 182
bussing, 19
Butcher, 16

C

Caesar, Julius, 167
Call parties, 75, 148, 183
Calvados, 166
captain, 17, 19, 50
Carême, (Marie-)Antonin, 7
Carson, Johnny, 3
cash register, 20
cashier, 17, 19, 20, 88
caterers, independent, 29
catering and sales managers, 29
Catskill Mountains, 1, 3
Caviar, 53, 125
Château Lafite-Rothschild, 170
chaud froids, 15
check average, 163
check holders, 36
Check presentation, 83, 87
Cheeses, Hard, 129
Cheeses, Soft, 129
chef, 4, 16, 21, 33, 40, 122, 123, 134,
    135, 146, 178, 180, 181
Chef Tournant
    Swing Cook, 16
Chef/Chefs, iii, 4, 5, 7, 10, 13, 15, 16,
    17, 23, 25, 29, 53, 72, 146, 155
children, 69, 131, 132, 133
Chivas Regal, 168
cigars, 19
Clearing the table, iv, 61, 90, 103-108
    When guests have vacated the table,
    107
    While guests are at the table, 105

Clos du Bois, 75
Cocktail Server, 20
cocktails, 21, 115
Cognac, 3, 19, 165
Comping food and beverage items,
    144, 183
complaints in restaurants, 6, 147
Complaints, guest, 154, 155
condiments, 63, 87, 91
convention and visitors' bureaus, 29
Conversation with co-workers, 39
Conversation with guests, 38
Coquille St. Jacques, 125
country clubs, 29
Courses of the meal, iv, 121, 124-129
    Appetizer, 125
    Beverages, 129
    Cheese and Fruit Course, 129
    Dessert Course, 128
    Entrée, 128
    Fish Course, 127
    Gourmandises. See Mignardises,
        Friandises, 129
    Salad Course, 127
    Sorbet, 128
    Soup, 126
cover, 16, 28, 32, 47, 68, 81, 96, 97, 98,
    100
Crumbing, 107
Cuisnier des rois et le roi des cuisniers,
    7
Culinary Arts Program, 4
Culinary Institute of America, 119
Culinary legends, iii, 7-11
culinary trends, 5

D

Dealing with guest problems, 153-157
Dealing with problem guests, 158-161
dietary concerns, 131, 133
Dining Room Manager, 109, 113
Dish Washer/Pot Washer, 17
dissatisfied customers, 153

Distillation, 164
Duck a l'Orange, 128
dupe, 45, 49

E

EATiQuette, ii, 4, a, b
  www.EATiQuette.com, 4
Escargot, 133
Escoffier, Auguste, 7, 8
Esquire Magazine, 3
Europe, 10, 23, 26, 99, 127
Executive Chef(s), 5, 14, 16

F

father of classic French cookery, 7
father of modern cooking, 8
Fermentation, 164
financial aspect of the job, 25
Fitzgerald, Ella, 3
flambé, 52
flatwares, 17
floral arrangements, 92
Foie Gras, 125
Food & Beverage Director(s), 18, 21,
  29
food and beverage consumption, 36
food service industry, 4, 29
Food Service Jobs
  Statistics, 23
Food temperatures, 53, 65, 78, 150
Ford, 4
Ford, President Gerald, 3
formal cuisine, 6
Foster's, 181
Framboise, 166
French cuisine, 8
French Service, 52
  Advantages, 53
  Disadvantages, 53
Friandises. See Gourmandises,
  Mignardises, 129

front and back of "house", 13-21
Front of House Job Descriptions, 18
Front-of-House, 10, 13, 17-21
Front-of-House flowchart, 18
Fry Cook, 15

G

Garde Manger, 15
General Manager, 18, 21
General Managers, 29
geriatrics, 131
Glassware (glasses), 17, 20, 21, 56, 58,
  61, 62, 64, 87, 91, 93, 95, 96, 98,
  99, 100, 103, 104, 105, 107, 122,
  132, 137, 138, 176, 188
Gluck, Etienne, 8
good will, 191
Goudeau, Emile, 124
Gourmandises. See Friandises,
  Mignardises, 129
Grand Marnier, 128, 166
Gravlox, 125
Greeting and seating, iv
guéridon, 52
Guerithault, Vincent, 3
guest check, 19, 26, 45
  Illustration, 79
guest check averages, 177
guest checks, 20, 71, 80
Guest dissatisfaction "tip-offs", 154
Guest problems, 153
Guest problems, dealing with, 153-157
  Apologize, 156
  Determine a solution, 157
  Follow-up, 157
  Listen, 156
  Notify manager, 157
guest who takes ill, 131
guests with a physical disability, 131

H

Hassayampa, 2
Havana Cafés, vi
Head Waiter, 9
Hearing impaired guests, 139
high profit margin, 163
Hilton, Conrad, 11
Hindus, 134
History Is Made At Night, 9, 42
Homer, 7
Hope, Bob, 3
Hops, 167
hors d'oeuvres, 15
host, iv, 9, 10, 11, 17, 50, 69, 71, 74,
    79, 83, 84, 88, 89, 108, 109, 118,
    119, 148, 173, 175, 176, 182, 190
Host/Hostess, 19
Host/hostess greeting, 83
Host/hostess responsibilities, 109-119
    Additional duties, 119
    Adjust the settings, 117
    Answering the phone, 111
    Creating balanced stations, 115
    Greeting the guest, 112
    Handing out menus, 118
    Leading the guest to the table, 116
    Maintaining a waiting list, 114
    Seating, 117
    Taking reservations, 109
Hostess, iv, 17, 40, 71, 83, 84, 90, 108,
    109, 110, 115, 117, 118, 119, 150,
    182, 183
hosts, iii, 7, 9, 11, 23, 182, 187
hotel chains, 29
Hug your guest, 58
human resource specialists, 32

I

ice carvings, 15
Inn of the Mountain Gods, 2
International Cuisine, 5

J

Jamaican rum, 165
Jamaican-style curried goat, 5
James Beard Foundation, 3
Japan, 178
Jews, 134

K

Kahlua, 166
Kamnitzer, Erasmo "Razz", 3
Keane, Edward, 9
Kendall Jackson, 181
King, B.B., 3
Kirsch, 165
kitchen hierarchy, 8
kitchen stations, 14, 80
Kitchen Steward, 17

L

Lambert, 4
Le Cirque, 10
Leftovers, 106
Lettuce Entertain You Enterprises, 10
Levy Restaurants, 187
Line Cooks, 15
linen, 20, 93
liqueurs, 19, 128
Liquor Service, 163
liquors, 163, 164, 168
Little Harbor Club, 2

M

Maccioni, Sirio, 10
Madison, President James, 167
Maître d' (Maître d'Hôtel), 1, 9, 10, 17,
    18, 19, 40, 109, 113, 182, 187
    Assistant Maître d', 3
Malt, 167
management schools and classes, 29

R

S

Veteran restaurateur and service instructor
David Rothschild *is available to present*

EATi&Quette^{SM}

waitstaff training and dining etiquette seminars
to your restaurant service team or culinary class

For information, please contact Barbara Rothschild
602.569.2051 • Fax: 602.765-1746 • info@EATiQuette.com
EATiQuette, 2238 E Wahalla Ln, Phoenix, AZ 85024-1260
or visit our Web site at: www.EATiQuette.com

NOTES:

Printed in the United States
19792LVS00002B/235-300

9 781591 130420